BEYOND BEYOND

70 RED HOT NEW POEMS

DENNIS DOPH

iUniverse, Inc.
NEW YORK BLOOMINGTON

BEYOND BEYOND
70 red hot new poems

iUniverse books may be ordered through booksellers or by contacting:

iUniverse
1663 Liberty Drive
Bloomington, IN 47403
www.iuniverse.com
1-800-Authors (1-800-288-4677)

Because of the dynamic nature of the Internet, any Web addresses or links contained in this book may have changed since publication and may no longer be valid.

ISBN: 978-1-4401-7293-9 (sc)
ISBN: 978-1-4401-7295-3 (hc)
ISBN: 978-1-4401-7294-6 (ebk)

Library of Congress Control Number: 2009935869

Printed in the United States of America

iUniverse rev. date: 9/1/2009

BEYOND BEYOND

In these times of tumult and of stress
Of perverse delights stumbled upon and found
Even wilder stuff discovered in duress
I'm inaugurating my new blog BEYOND BEYOND
Since I'm pushing into my seventh decade
Enough experience to capitulate or capture
Still pushing out at the head of this Pig Parade
Pushing my anal ring out of my aperture
Pushing what little male beauty I have left
Beyond the contrapuntal moral shift
Beyond the pain of those who are bereft
Beyond the comfort of a Botox lift
Encourage Bear Men to lick the sperm
  From my red fur
Clean me like an old tomcat from my positions
  Heinous
Remembering my former flexibility
  As it were
Puckering my well regarded wide pink anus
Savoring the last ejaculation on my lips
That male protein of which I am so fond
Applying vitamin E to my poor bruised
   nips
Offering myself up for BEYOND BEYOND

As Cheney swivels as he will and must
Pursuing every opportunity to justify
The heartbreaking breach of faith and trust
Stuck like a dirty thumb in our collective eye
Snarling like a shark drunk with the blood of others
Steeped in his brothers' blood in the shrinking tide
Snapping like a rabid spaniel
   At McCain's and others' mothers
All I can think of beside (beside)
Is the absurdist world of Beyond (Beyond)

1

Where Eric Cantor shinnies up to every stud in heat
Where that bitch from Alaska is everything
        Of which I am not fond
Where Bush dies like a mangy dog at our feet
Because we offered ourselves up to these
        Mothergrabbers
Because we forced ourselves to believe
        They were not lying
These lousy, cynical, blood-addled
        Sharks and scabbers
I could off any one of them without even
        Trying
And yet we comfort ourselves with our little
        Golden Man
Exhausted, bent, perpetually stooped
Unable to experience emotion other than
What it is like to be terminally *pooped*

And yet; (and yet) we go sailing into the
        Golden Dawn
Of Shittybank and Skank of America
Calculating which lousy investment we have
        Yet to lose upon
Putting our loose change on this country
        Win, lose or draw

LABELS

We live our entire lives with conventient labels

Some of them are legal
   Some of them are moral
      Some of them are patriotic
         Some of them are narcissistic
            Some of them are sentimental

Once I was legally a CHILD   Hated every moment of it
Hated being a child   Hated being thought of as a child
Even in the days when I only came up to a full grown man's
   Belly button
Later I saw dwarves giving full grown men blowjobs
   From that position
Realized what an opportunity I had missed   When the CHILD
Label prevented me from some serious
   Hanky-panky

Morally as a CHILD I was beyond reproach   Actually
   I was a very nasty child
My cousin Steve and I thought of several juicy things
   To say
About our Grandmother's Navy Mothers kaffee klatsch
Their grey beards sometimes tweezed   sometimes
   Depilitorized
Never escaped our attention   What cruddy conservative
   Old men these old women were
Steve and I never tired of finding ways to humiliate
   And degrade
These nasty old women with their sensible shoes
Their husbands frequently tried to fondle us
We were beautiful children   Much too beautiful
Certain of the randy old men who tried to show us their
   Priceless treasures
Which they kept in their pockets   We were expecting

Candy   We got the big drooling head
Of a dick   Here the MORAL question kicked in
We could have told the Old Hens their husbands
        Were busy showing little kids their dicks
What they were doing was IMMORAL   besides
        The old bitches would have found a way
        To side with their husbands   Suddenly
WE would have been the culprits   WE would have been
        IMMORAL   Another convenient label

We faced the PATRIOTIC or UNPATRIOTIC label
When we were very little children   we learned
Our grandfather   Our uncles and the mother of one of us
        Mine to be exact
Had supported the Liberal (Communist) side in the
        Spanish War
Now red baiters in Washington State were pillorying
        Our family
Steve and I were suspect   More than suspect
We were Reds   We learned to carry the burden of another
        Generation's political convictions
At a time when a mealy mouthed old ex general
        Was President of these United States
Reds were being run out of the movie business   Reds
        Were being run out of politics
My mother was replaced on the Washington State
        Democratic National Committee
By an asskissing friend of Senator Jackson   Another
        War hawk
We were outsiders and UNPATRIOTIC   Naturally
        We were on the greased slide
        To be BAD   Another convenient label

 Steve and I entered the amazing world of NARCISSISM
A label that came at us right out of left field   When Steve discovered
        (Tiny little guy scarcely more than five feet tall)
Discovered he was carrying around a piece of meat

Any truck driver would have given his left nut to sport
   About a year later
 Found out I had one of those too
Much to the horror and fascination of our less fortunate cousins
   Who didn't
So we lived for our dicks   Hey   We were BAD   We were
   UNPATRIOTIC
We were no longer children   we were fair game   We were
   TEENS   In the Sixties that meant something shocking
You were either Tab Hunter or James Dean and
   Nothing in between
Later when Steve and I found out what absolute perverts
   Tab Hunter and James Dean were
We laughed   The label was conflated   BAD TEENS
   GOOD TEENS
All up the waterspout

Worst of all the SENTIMENTAL label   GOOD SON
   HONORABLE FATHER
   DOTING MOTHER
   LOVING GRANDMOTHER
   SUPPORTIVE AUNTS UNCLES AND COUSINS
All of that was put to the test   Found very much wanting
I was as good as I could be until I learned I was way smarter
   Than either of my parents Which I discovered
When I was about four   My mother was borderline crazy
Sometimes   Not even so borderline   My father
   Was unforgiveably naïve
So the meanings of those labels were challenged   Then:
   LOVING GRANDMOTHER
Had already taken its toll when I found she'd frozen her very
   Interesting husband
Out of her emotions but not her life   SUPPORTIVE ETC
   Fell by the wayside too
Leaving me in New York in the late 60s   Very alone
With all my labels scattered about me like ratty parade banners
   After the parade had gone by

Then I discovered another label: TOP
  Worked for me for thirty-five years. Still
  Working on it

I SEARCHED FOR MY MUSE

I searched for my Muse when inspiration went dry
Thought he was located in the Sweet Bye-and-Bye
But when the clouds of Parnassus were drawn
There was my perky Muse sitting upon
A big ivory dildo shaped like a fist
So I left him squatting there in the mist
Like a hairy-assed concupiscent imp
And my inspiration, like my dick, went limp.

I searched for my Muse in Great Literature
Plodding through libraries I was more than sure
That I was on the right aesthetic track
In pursuing Proust or Colette – or Balzac.
When I got to the third volume of Monsieur P
I found where my Muse just had to be
Like the leaders of Proust's forgotten French nation
He was suffering the agonies of degradation
So with each new stroke of the proverbial flogger
I was turning into a lazy blogger

I searched in Great Cinema for my Muse of yore
Wandering where I had never gone before
Suffering through Resnais whom I found quite phony
And the icy surfaces of Antonioni
Finally in Ingmar Bergman my Muse was espied
In the hell of *Cries and Whispers* no feeling denied
Ingrid Thulin was the Sultana of Swat
When she shoved that broken champagne glass
        Up her lubricated twat
So when Ingrid took a break for one well-earned pee
My Muse once again revealed himself to me

I investigated myself in a full length mirror
Wondering whether my fugitive Muse
        Was *here ....or here .... Or here*

My bushy armpits were an illogical site
Found cooties on my chest   Could go on
        Searching all night
For the Elusive Muse who was not up my nose
Not down my throat or anywhere in my clothes
Finally I rolled up on my Yoga pumped shoulders
Aching from the flogger like parallel boulders
Spread my butt cheeks so I could see my anus
Suddenly in a manner more than heinous
My Muse appeared in the crack of my butt
Grinning like Satan and saying,   *"You slut,*
You better crank that big Kraut dick and prepare
        To forgive
Your elusive Muse since THIS is where I live …!"

So I'm alerting the gentlemen who want much more of me
Like the Elusive Muse
        You have to go for the Core of Me

CRUNCH CRUNCH YUMMMMMMM

I am Antonia. I'm a tiger fifteen years old
Famous for my temper and my beauty
I live in a cage in San Francisco Zoo
They treat me allright   Once in awhile
The keepers forget that I am Antonia
I give them a good reason to remember
I bite. After all I am a tiger   I belong
In the Jungle in China or maybe Laos
Maybe both   I don't belong here

Sometimes they give me raw red meat
Torn off one of their tame barnyard animals
That's Ok   I wish there was bone on it
I fantasize the bone while I crunch the tame
Animal meat of the cow or the horse or the bull

Crunch Crunch Yummmmmmmmmmm

Couple of weeks ago one of the keepers
Made the mistake of kicking me while he
Prodded me from my cage out into the open air pen
     Where they make us spend the day
Natives of San Francisco and tourists come there
They scream at us and taunt us
Throw stupid shit at us   Popcorn   Applecores
Dumb shit like that   The keeper gave me
A sound kick while I was going through
The gate   Waited till he had his back turned
When I was safely outside   Then I bit his fat Dago ass
     He wasn't sure which of us did it
We were all snarling   After all we are tigers
Spent the rest of the day in a tree   Savoring
The experience

Crunch Crunch Yummmmmmmmmmmmm

Today has been especially trying   It's Saturday
A day all of us dread   They prod us out into
The pen earlier than usual   Feed us small rations
Green shit rather than red meat to keep us
Hungry and active   Little Chicano kids
Come into the Zoo around ten   They all carry
Crappy candy in wrappers   Fruit from home
Sometimes the little bastards throw the candy
Still in the wrappers at us   Fuck how I hate them
Around eleven three full grown Mexican guys
Came up against the pit surrounding the pen
We could tell they were bombed   They had
Noisy Mexican cowboy music on their IPods
      Singing   Shrieking taunts at us
In Spanish   One of the guys threw a rock at me
Instead of an apple   Just for the hell of it I ate
The rock   Then when he was balanced up against
The edge of the pit I decided, What the Hell
I made the jump I had always decided I could make
If I got mad enough   I was mad enough

Crunch Crunch Yummmmmmmmmmmmmm

ANSWER TO WHY IS NOTHING

Tonight driving home in a snazzy rented BMW
My partner elated by the smooth management
Of the vehicle   the fact steroid injections
Are ironing out the terrible pain in his spine
Told me, our beefy little Iranian doctor had asked him
    Why
He hadn't come in to be checked out as he should
And his answer was
    Nothing
Since it was apparent to both of them This guy
Only goes to the doc when he damn well needs to
They both know it

Amazing
How often this dictum applies to the shit you do
In your life   My mother asked
    Why
Did her brothers and sisters   Her brothers' and sisters'
Children avoid her   When they knew she was crazy
As a bedbug in mating season   She knew it   They knew it
So the answer to that was Nothing

She was flipped out but still had to ask
    Why

My Dad asked over and over again
    Why
Did his fat German sister and her Disney-animal loving
Norwegian husband retreat from life as anyone knew it
My dad began to mourn Blanche before she even croaked
They lived for and with each other for each delicious meal
Blanche cooked till they both ate themselves into a sugar
Induced coma

When Blanche and Stogie finally croaked months apart

He kept on asking
        Why
But the answer of course was
        Nothing   Blanche and Stogie enjoyed working
Their mandibles till they shoveled dirt over them

My Grandmother asked querulously   tears in her pale
Blue eyes
        Why
Did she take the trouble to carry fourteen argumentative
Irish children to full term then urge them through their
Childhoods   Expecting always receiving the kind of
Chronic disappointment they meted out to her
        So she got Nothing
But the bitter gall tasting disappointment she always knew
Would be on her plate

Both of my parents fed up as they were
With their frustrating maddening lives where nothing
Ever worked out right   Waited with baited breath
For me to be devastated   How I would respond
To the savage dismissal of Me by the World at Large
When the World at Large realized I was about 150% gayer
Than I needed to be   They waited in their separate beds
In their separate bedrooms waiting for me to scream
        Why
It's been a long fruitless wait   Never rewarded them
With my silent scream   For me that was a big Nothing
 I'm totally at ease with myself   Either on my feet
Or on my knees   So that's a big Nothing
        ....isn't it?

BORING OLD MEN

Oh John
Your face is the blasted face of the old Nam vets
Remembering the Hanoi Hilton which no one forgets
Endless war is your aim   Just another Point of Hate
With Iraq poised to become the 51st state
War Hawks think you are heaven sent
But you'd turn out to become our *very oldest* President
Though Ronnie was old you are even older
With a tic in your face and a chip on your shoulder

> *Boring old men   Boring old men*
> *America 2000 is beyond your ken*
> *You're still firing off your blunderbusses*
> *Lifting your dead genitals into your trusses*
> *And the last man I would want to lean upon*
> *Is swollen faced apoplectic Boring Old John*

Oh Mitt
You handsome weasel you   There's nothing in your mind
Nothing but winning   Lying   Pretending to the broke
Auto workers of Michigan you are one
        Of their kind
But you act like you're suffering from a terminal stroke
You'd give the Detroit mavins a long free ride
With a jobless union membership clinging to your side
You lied about your dad marching with Martin Luther King
But we all know you'll lie about anything
Hoping we'll all forget you were the Governor of Mass
Picking South Carolina gravel out of your ass

> *Boring old men   Boring old men*
> *You lie and steal and waffle and then*
> *You borrow the mantle of Ronnie so Dear*
> *Even though it's sufficiently clear*
> *None of you has the power to unite*

A fucked-up party with your old man's bite
So pack your five perfect boys into your
        Old Detroit car
And send them to the nearest Michigan
        Gay bar

Oh Rudy
As much as you hold aloft precious memories
Of New York
We know how much you're really hated there
Japping out on the Fireman's union after
        Four months of disgusting work
Freezing even Brooklynites with your icy
        Sicilian stare
Dismissing your second wife with a press
        Conference
Pretending the first one never existed
Marrying a third one without a shred of
        Common sense
And now, in your *folie du grandeur,*
        You've insisted
That since you were On the Ground at 9/11
You are the logical substitute for the Son of Heaven
You scrounge from primary to primary
        Looking for a place to sit
You're the logical substitute for nothing but shit

    Boring old Men Boring old Men
    Nothing like playing the Fear Card again
    No point remembering how you left New York
        A mess
    How your gay friends on the East Side
    Duded you up in a dress
    Even though you play hide-the-sausage
        With that old tart Judy
    There's nothing more boring than boring old
        Rudy

Oh Fred
Served one undistinguished term as the Senator from Tenn
Making all Tennesseans wish they'd never see you
       Again
Spent four seasons showing off your rubbery
       Public face
Showing commercial television a more than usual
       Disgrace
You troll your tired old body into the Killing Field
You sure can't run   You can magnificently yield
You're taller than most   You're old and stout
You're totally out to lunch   Completely zoned out
But in the Republican scheme you're like every mom's son
Loyal stupid predictable Fred Thompson

> *These old farts are so infinitely boring*
> *But this one has me yawning and snoring*
> *The Leadership Bit at least he can fake*
> *But he has this problem about staying awake*

Oh Mike
Youngest of the lot but still older than old
Instead of running hot you're running ice cold
Even the evangelicals seem to have your number
As you drive old dead Dixie back into her slumber
You proved your minions were totally corrupted
When you got on about that Indian kid
       McCain adopted
Only one one issue have you not come a cropper
You taught us how to make squirrel stew
       In a popcorn popper

> *Oh, boring, boring, boring old men*
> *You're all meditation   Absolutely no Zen*
> *Don't have the juice for spittin' but you sure are*
>   *Hawkers*

You're all in a race – a race for your walkers
So in 2008 it's compulsively strange
When we hear the old Eisenhower mantra:
   It's time for a change

KARMIC CONUNDRUM

It's a conundrum   My two greatest strengths
        Are what I have above my shoulders
        And what I have below my waist
When most men find out about the brain part
        They are prepared to depart in haste
They love meditating on my dick
        Or my big broad chest all covered
        With red fleece
But when they find out I'm an intellectual
        They squeeze out of my space
        Like pigs covered with grease
Only the *rara avis* man   The one who can operate
        With more than half a brain
Is the one who can contemplate both my halves
        The dick one and the brain one
        Without going slightly insane
So when you guys who flip out
        When you see me parading around
        With a big hard-on
            and a leather halter
Find out about my disturbing brain
        It's the rare bird who goes on
        To celebrate the brain with me
            Without fail and without falter
So yes my friends
        You can get down on me
        You can stroke my sphincter
            With your callous mitts
But the kind of man I really want
        Is the man who can blow my brain to bits
I really want a sexy brainy man
        Who has the balls to celebrate my soul
Not a boy man who runs from Marcel Proust
        And fades away to watch the Superbowl
So when you encounter this Karmic Conundrum

Known far and wide as Dennis Doph
Just be prepared to jack my brain up
    As well as being first in the queue
        To jack me off

THE SHELF

I'm not ready to be put on the shelf
I'm not ready to put myself on the shelf
I've been on the shelf. It's lonely there
Climbed onto the shelf when my docs set me up
For my handy dandy colonoscopy
      All of their damned loopy procedures
Their little electric mouse sucked out half of my guts
Left the other half which barely work
      Still undaunted
Refuse to take up my Senior Citizen place on the shelf
Guys look at me every day like they want to grab some
Walk with it shoved forward so they can see
      What they'd like to grab
Still a damn fine handful I can assure you
Yesterday the handsome bear of a New Mexico Indian
      From Yogalab
The guy who keeps proclaiming he hates sex
Came onto me in the dressing room pressing his
      Lubricated nips into both of my hands
      If this is how he hates sex
 I'd like to see what he's like
When he decides he loves it
Passed him by   I can do better than that
Much better
Have my own NewMex guy with his wavy hair
      And his square shoulders
Waiting for us to give each other a mutual fingerwave
And that stupendously hot Muscledad with his
      Thick black beard
      Hanging his sling from the ceiling
And of course, always
That handsome Hound of Hell in Brazil
Offering his pelt as a secret place for me
      To hide myself in
No I will not put myself on the shelf   Despite

Random cocked-up opinions that I belong there
Where I belong is where I can work
    And be worked on
    When I'm really old
I can look back at my passionate priapic life
    And say to myself
"Well, stud, at least you didn't put yourself
    on the shelf too soon".

SO WHAT IF

So what if
My memory bank is broke
And my shirts are never starched
And I mistake my talcum for a toot of coke
And my throat is always parched
And my butt is numb from sitting all day
On this endless Internet chair
And most of the men that I meet this way
Blow me off while I'm sitting there
So what if
My red hair isn't quite real
And one shoulder is higher than the other
And I never scored men who could make me feel
Like the men who scored with my mother
And most of my pretensions are really ersatz
Designed to lift me another notch
And if my pajamas are not really the cat's
And they bind in my busy old crotch
And my balls have gone from fat plums to chandeliers
And my chest hair from brick red to hoar
And I'm tired of messing with these tweaked little dears
And pretending that less is more
Oh so what if
My waist is getting a wee bit stout
And my silver has turned to tin
And that Bush is really on his way out
And SHE is on her way in*
So what if I count my detractors in the dozens
With few admirers to replenish my soul
So what if I resemble the least of my cousins
On the wrong side of a public-accomodation hole
But I still get admirably astoundingly hard
And rip holes in my 501s
And my nipples lead my way into a room
Those adventurous son of a guns

So if I continue to be kind of wild
And get even more bang for my buck
I will venture to muse that my Inner Child
Is a mean little son of a fuck

WHO THEY ARE

If who they are is what they say they are
They should get what they want
       Without even trying
But if who they are is what I think they are
They can go on playing Mary Five Fingers
       'cause they are lying

If who they are is what they used to be
And what they are now
       Is a shadow of doubt
What they used to be is probably
       Bupkis
And I'd rather hear them whisper
       Than stand and shout

If who they are is what they might become
Well, hell: who can afford to stand
       Around and wait?
If what they might become is just
       More attitude and beef
Then they can stack that beef
       On someone else's plate

If what I am seems like a little bit
Just not worth mentioning
       Or even pumping
Just flip my switches *once*
       To get the most of it
And find a new meaning for hedonism
       Or flat out humping

If what we might become
Is just so much hot air
So much hyperbole or feckless hyping
I should just bail out

Of the Catbird chair
And use these five fingers for something else
      Besides typing

So if who they are depends
      Upon what I am
I'd say the fire that's burning
      Is so much char
But if what I am
      Really makes them give a damn
Then I'll shout, *"God-damn, Sam!"*
      For who they are

DEW DROP INN

Welcome to Dew Drop Inn
From five to nine
Where the boys in lace-up jockstraps lurk seductively
Where men clad only in Army boots bark out instructively
    "Use that fist, Stud Boy!!"
    Act just like an Army trucker
Or a bulldyke   In lipstick lesbo mode
Where you use your lips as suction cups
    And your penis for a goad
Yeah the air is thin in Dew Drop Inn
    And the Crisco runs like wine
    In the Posing Chair you can just sit there
Dew Drop Inn   It's really fine

Check in to Dew Drop Inn
It's really unnaturally choice
Watch that big blond stud in leather bind his balls
As his partner sucks the other hunks in toilet stalls
    The excitement is right in his hands
    As he shoots saline right into his glans
And the vanilla guy from Valley Village
Morphs into a Stud Top in this constant
    Sexual pillage
In this hot thin air they slip their jocks off
And the dwarf from *Pirates of the Caribbean*
    Gets his rocks off

Learn the Finer Facts at Dew Drop Inn
Yeah   The Finer Facts of Fisting
Has each tweaked studboy enlisting
    And it's truly tweakedly vexing
    When these brain-damaged boys can't learn
    The finer points of finger flexing
It's Second Sphincter City at Dew Drop Inn
    When each new recruit shouts, *"Hell, Beau,*

Push your digits to the elbow"
And your fingers get so damned swollen
You just have to cool 'em off
        In the transverse colon

Halfway down the block from Dew Drop Inn
You can smell the stench of leaking
Anal chambers and the creaking
        Of a fine duet of slings
        And other more lethal things
Suddenly out of the haze   We see old Van Johnson
        From Metro days
Like Marley's Ghost of Yore   He's the Fisting Ghost
        Of Christmas Past   Gone way before
And lo! With her bulldog jaw   Here's little Debbie
        With her ruff randy   *"RAH! RAH! RAH!"*
        Johnson and Keenan Wynn jig a wild *Erin Go-Bragh*

        And the Maitresse of Dew Drop Inn
        Ace fellatrix Nancy Davis
        Had her personal troupe of slaves
So shoot the saline to your peter
And beat the fatal fisting meter
        It's all theater

GRADUALLY, BY DEGREES

Oh I will be so good
So very very good
I will respect my elders
And try so very hard to please
I'll tip my hat to old women
If I ever wear a hat
 I'll shake hands heartily with all the old cockers
          And smile like I have just said "Cheese".
I'll laugh at the rudest jokes
And pretend pop culture is significant
I'll ignore all the rants of Republicans
And the tight mean looks on their faces
Yes I will do all these things
When the moon has a face like Lou Costello
And Pope Benedict struts in a pink bikini
….gradually. By degrees.

I'll be effervescently happy
Not sanguine
          Or silly or stolid

I'll drive the latest dumb-ass car
And install all the dumbed-out extras
I'll be just as good as I can possibly be
In this new Jesus Phase of my existence
I'll open the door for Hillary Clinton
Instead of slamming it in her face
I'll work out seven days a week
And never again touch ice cream
Yes, I will do all these things
All these terrible noble things
And I won't expect praise or even contentment
….gradually. By degrees

I'll play video games with my kid cousins

I'll pretend I don't want to kick Miley Cyrus
I'll go to every God-damned Harry Potter movie
I'll say loudly that they're simply wonderful
I'll stop watching foreign language movies
Because it is so very American to hate them
I'll give a tip to the wetback who delivers
      The paper
For throwing it like a bomb against the door
I'll never watch another Woody Allen movie
I'll pay a very heavy price for all this virtue
But I'll do it all so gradually
So very, very gradually
You might not even know it's happening

As I avoid all my kid cousins
Kick Miley Cyrus in her fat kid rump
Avoid (as I have, up to this time)
Every God-damned Harry Potter movie
I'll be the first four-eyed intellectual in line
For every subtitled movie that opens
I'll scream at the wetback who delivers the paper
And threaten to report him to Immigration
Because I am a bad, bad boy
Been a bad, bad boy for a very long time
Because I love it
I indubitably outrageously *love it*
But I will (as I said) slowly change
To be a big dicked embodiment of Mother Teresa
I *will* change. I *will*. I *will*.
Oh so gradually. Very gradually.
      Imperceptibly gradually. By degrees.

CELLTSURIS

Goddamn it I am a man of a certain age
Desperately selfish about his privacy
Walking around firmly on two flat feet
Ready to kick ass when my privacy is invaded
Flirted briefly

With the idea of carrying a cellphone
I'm as good as married to another old fart
With a big dick We communicate with each other
Very well thank you Everywhere I go
I see

Screamin nannies Cleaning women
Six months ago they were shoveling donkey shit
In Colima Now pushing megastrollers
Very white children who are not related to them
Inside

The old cunt with the megastroller is calling
Her granddaughter in Colima advising her
On her Quinceana rite   Sit sipping my latte
On Larchmont Boulevard See and hear women
Who have been friends

Since they plagued Sister Mary Agnes
At Immaculate Heart cellphoning each other
They are sitting fifteen feet away from each other
Both experiencing the pain of premature menopause
Pantygirdles

Chafing their precious pussies While they cellphone
To the max Meanwhile their husbands are probably
Out cellphoning the chickiebods they're balling
Better still some Yogabuddy of mine whose dick
Has wakened

A new sense of involvement in this pussy whipped
Scoundrel Serenely drift by all this celltsuris
Serene in my majestic aloneness Pulling down my
Splendid Territory Ahead mustard colored pants
Which I ordered

Online Showing you the best butt on the Pacific
Seaboard Mooning you Telling you Take your cell
And shove it

In Montenegro Europe's latest instant republic
Newly sprung forth from the wreckage of the former
Yugoslavia No one has a land line All those fucking
Meiskeits have cells They are talking talking
Talking talking

On a fast track to EU membership Eurail is routing
The old Berlin to Baghdad express through Montenegro
Serbia will be the Bad Boy of Europe forever
These goddamned hairy half Serbian half Bosnian
Nosepickers

Can eat their cells Literally shove their fucking
Cells up their noses They can vault into the EU
Which has a much better economy than poor
Impoverished Jesusland I'm very tall Very handsome
Verging on Old

The only thing I need a cellphone for is to pack it
Into your ass like a tampon So you can pick up
Police calls on your transverse colon

STORY ENTICER

I am the Story Enticer
Like the spider at the core of his web
   Spin and lure, spin and lure, to be sure
I am the boy who used to cause steel-ripping
    automobile accidents
Walking the streets of Seattle in cutoff shorts
The legs are just as good now   Oh so many years later
The stuff in the shorts is just as good now   Maybe better

My grand-dad was a Story Enticer
Lean old hairy Mediterranean-looking Irishman
Looking down his long old lean-Irish nose at me
     Which I inherited
He told stories of his boyhood in rural Maine
How bad he was   Always such a bad boy Always in trouble
I adored grand-dad   Even when I knew he was lying

His daughter Doris was a bulldyke who was a Story Enticer
In Hollywood she kept a collection of women
   on their way down
And women on their way up
And plush puppy former leading men   All entranced
With her improbable imponderable stories   When all they wanted
   Was a taste of her amazing female-ness
Smoldering there between her legs

Played four handed Canasta with Grand-dad and Doris
And my very plain very frightened Grandma
Who knew Will and Doris were lying but she kept her counsel
   And listened listened listened and cried cried cried
And kept the candle burning in the window
Usually partnered with Doris and we won
Grand-dad would throw his cards across the room
Then Doris would take me out to the gay bars of Seattle
   Tacoma and Everett

Where we would sing Marlene Dietrich songs   I was six

Later when I was twelve I would sing Marlene Dietrich songs
With the appropriate moves   The dykes loved it

I was a Story Enticer in high school   Always too aware
Of my budding very long very lean body
Always covered up to the neck down to the wrists
Still they tried to peel me like an onion
        Sometimes I let them Oh yeah   I let them
        Sometimes they paid a price for peeling me
Growing up in the 1960s was hard for a big handsome
Red-headed boy of a certain persuasion
Who would allow himself to be persuaded
    Under the right circumstances
And under many of the wrong ones

In college I was a Story Enticer
Covered the theatre beat for the college newspaper
Allowed myself to be sucked into the local theater scene
Suddenly Seattle had discovered nudity
And me all in one fell swoop   I was Lodowick in
        Christopher Marlowe's *Jew of Malta*
Suddenly all of Seattle was aware of my beautiful
        Callipyginous ass and my perfectly formed youngman's
            Penis
    There they were all cooing and gasping
A star was born
        And he was worn like the Victorian *September Morn*
    This year's fashion in yesterday's shocking nudity

Moved to New York in '68   Running out of scores
        In rainy Seattle
My poor love besotted Cherokee house mate driven mad
        With frustration
    Flaming through the streets of Manhattan
        Flaming flaming like my ass was on fire

32

It was only youth and a lot of bullshit
>   Went on flaming flaming and like moths drawn to the flame

Young Jews and Puerto Ricans and *Oh God the Italians*
All drawn to my Pillar of Fire
We were twisting the night away
Men drawn to men over and over again
>   *Over and over and over again with hundreds*
>   *Of sex besotted men*
>   *And the occasional woman drawn to the muscular*
>   *Group grope*
>   *Running out of patience   and hope*

Finally I became the Story Enticer for that groaning old
>   Major Studio

One that told the best of stories in the worst of times
Selling their past   The best of their past
No one needs to be a genius to sell Rita Hayworth
Met her when she was just manifesting the true symptoms
>   Of the Alzheimer's which killed her

Still she was beautiful thin and needed to dance
She moved like she was the greatest dancer in the world
>   But had forgotten how

She was blind as a bat   We led her around by her
>   Pinkly manicured hands   and loved her

Loved Cary and Burt and many of the Good Old Boys too
>   But in a different much more memorable way

Now I've moved into different realm of Story Enticing
Like Rita my feet have stopped dancing
>   But my eyes are still telling the same old story
>   My hands are telling that story too   in Braille
>   The kind of Braille none of you will forget

INSATIABLE

I am insatiable for Rum Raisin Haagen-Dasz
It has laid waste to the waist that was
And even though I do curls and situps till
    I faint
The Haagen-Dasz makes the distance between
    The bulky bear I am
    And the slim otter I ain't

I am insatiable for the opera diva Debbie Voigt
Dropping 150 pounds she has become a beauty
    Quite
Like Renee Fleming with warmth; or like
    Maria Callas
Without the restraining 150 pounds of ballast

I'm insatiable for furry little Sergi Lopez
One look at that fur bearing animal and my
    Heart says *yezzzzzzzzzzzzzzzz*
Sergi turns my penis into one huge sperm
    Producing plinth
And sucks me deep into *Pan's Labyrinth*

What really piques my hunger and insatiability
Is the Right Wing of this country with its
    Arrogance and incivility
I cannot wait to give them the last electoral push
With confidence we never again elect
    Anyone named Bush

I'm insatiable for each large cut or uncut penis
None of these items should come between us
Short of my insatiable need to bare one
I have no problem with this concept: *share one.*

I'm not insatiable for cunts
But I was once

DESERTED

My Muse has deserted me
He's gone on down the Street With No Name
He's peddling his ass to bullyboys
Selling out
        Without any sense of shame
My Muse doesn't give a shit
        For my personal quest
He's quit me before I begged him to quit
Selling his artistic soul to Reader's Digest

My Muse has Japped out on me
He's pulled up his trousers and split
        The scene
Telling all my detractors I have no talent
And that I'm unequivocally mean
He's unconditionally deprecating
Of my quirks and my quest
And to make things even more humiliating
        He's shaved his chest

My Muse left the orgy before I did
While I was still strapped up in the sling
He slid in the Crisco and while he slid
He cried out
        "This fucker is not worth anything!"
And I'm not going to beg him
        Not to desert me
Or go on my knees to implore him
        To come back
My Muse is a skanked-out tattooed fucktop
        Wasted on crack

BACK OFF

The Dirty Minded Guy and his Dirty Minded Friends
Paired off over a sling-based resolution
This filthy minded Slut is not all that he pretends
As the Slut's Filthy Friends abjure bathing or ablution
But what really turned the Dirty Minded Guy off
      Big time
Is when the Handsome Old Guy tried to spank his butt
      Peppermint pink
Told the Handsome Old Guy to back off of that smut
And go stick his head in the kitchen sink

> *Back off! No one touches this man's backside*
> *With anything save venal lust or pride*
> *And no one better try to spread it wide*
>   *With malice and malingerers*
> *I may be quite obviously bent*
> *Extremely strong in Tremor of Intent*
> *Unfortunately the places I frequent*
>   *Are full of fumblers and fingerers*

The Dirty Minded Guy ambled down to New Mex
Checked out the scene   Checked out the supple studs thereto
Ate a breakfast consisting of piss and Wheat Chex
Then tried to find what serious New Mex studs do
The best of them had hands the size of baseball mitts
Which made the Dirty Minded Guy feel shivery and slimy
Then the New Mex Stud pulled a trick which was the pits
And tried to shove those mitts right up our hero's heinie

> *Back off, stud! You might be handsomer than most*
> *In Santa Fe you present a perfect host*
> *But if you try to fist me you'll be toast*
>   *The source of retching*
> *I hear these Sex Studs with their boos and hisses*
> *It's my intent to seriously augment their blisses*

But my poor backside knows what a trial this is
…. anal stretching

Once in awhile we visit the site known as ASSPIG
Crooning with lust over these furry fellas
Communicating with 'em makes It swells so very big
That my ejaculation rate requires umbrellas
So we eyeball this furry beast in Silverlake
Who eyeballs back the Dirty Minded Mouth
      To hump in
This Furry Beast is really pretty hard to take
Because he views that rosy mouth as something new
      To take a dump in

      Back off, furry stud! I can't be humped to pieces
      Even though your fur quotient my pulse increases
      I'm not a repository for foreign feces
          So just stop talking
      Back off! I know for me what Wrong or Right is
      Can't think of anything which more tasteless
          Or more trite is
      And I shall not exit this mortal plane
          Ravaged by Heptatitis
          So keep on walking

MY SENIOR PROM

My Senior Prom turned into an interesting rout.
I'd been dating this goodlooking piano-playing
Cutie pie *Lily Jaeger,* for two years. We had
No sexual vibe of any kind, unlike myself and
Some fish

In my senior class. If I was attracted to women
At all, it was adult women. Lil catered to the
Baby in me. She brought chicken lunches to
School and treated me like I needed my ass wiped.
I did

But not by her. It was a given Lil & I would be
One hot date at the Prom. Another cuddlin' couple were
Bound to be *Vern Akkich* and *Anita Dollefson.*
Vern was the captain of the Queen City Football Team.
Six-three, 200 lbs.

Thick black hair, shoulders like a landing pad
For a B-17, dimples. Anita he'd knocked up
Halfway through our junior year. She'd just
Given birth to a strapping baby boy, after dropping
Out of High

After the first quarter of her senior year. Anita
Was very pretty, very blond, with big tits and now,
Nursing, even bigger ones. When Vern and I
Double dated, Anita let me milk her. Human milk
Tastes a little

Like Carnation Condensed but bitter. Passed on it
The second time she offered it. Lil was a bit of an
Uptight citizen,   closet Sapph to my knowledge.
Had one redheaded female cousin who cultivated
The Sapph side,

They all regarded Lil as a promising convert. We
Double-dated the Prom as well. Vern and I were
Resplendent in our rented tuxes, Lil wore midnight
Blue with irridescents, quite mature, good for
Piano concerts.

Anita was in pink as usual, which was just right
For a pretty Norwegian girl with big micturating
Tits.

The third dance we were all given a chance to
"change partners". I danced with Anita, Vern
with Lil. Then without warning, we swapped again.
I danced with Vern. A collective gasp of supershock
Went up

In the surrounding arena. They knew we were both
Capable of pushing the envelope, but no one was
Prepared for two big handsome boys, pushing their
Crotches together, arms around each other, lips on
Each other's necks.

Particularly when one was the editor of the school
Paper and the other the captain of the football team.

Lil and Anita danced together. Lil put her hands
On both of Anita's big leaking tits. I could see Lil
Was going into Hog Heaven as she let voluptuous
Anita grab both cheeks of her ass as they danced.
Lucky Lil was wearing midnight blue.

We left the Prom after that third dance. Anita took
The wheel and Lil settled in beside her, never even
Glancing at me and Vern in the back seat. Lil went
Down on Anita while she drove the streets of Queen
City, having one orgasm after another

As Lil ate out her twat. Vern and I were necking up
A storm in the back seat; hauled out Vern's thick
Croatian dick and began to suck it. Lil just reared up,
Glanced at us once, and went back to the heaven
She had found in Anita's crotch.

I never dated Lil again. Vern and I were a de facto
Couple for the rest of my senior year, frequently having
Three-ways with the co-captain of the football team, one
Lenny de Mettre who was a screamin' hunk with thick
Black hair and blue eyes.

My redheaded semi-Sapph cousin told me that both
Lenny and Vern were fat wrecks at our fortieth anniversary
Graduation ceremony. Even though I had been the editor
Of the school paper, I did not attend the event. I never
Saw Vern again

After we graduated. Lenny and I got it on several times
Through the years following but I haven't seen
Or touched him since I moved to New York
In 1968. We were three hunky boys with big dicks
Celebrating something very special . Now they
Are grandfathers and

I am me. Lil went totally Sapph; Anita divorced
Vern after three years of unhappy marriage to morph
To another and then another alcoholic heterosexual
Marriage. Finally she joined Lil on the Sapph side
For good.

They are now in their late fifties living together
On the ocean side of Camano Island, raising spit
Babies. The big baby boy Anita had out of wedlock
Is now forty-one.

Time, you harlot!

LUCY JADE

Time I addressed the memory of the foul female animal
        Lucy Jade
Out of the farming flats of Fresno   playing the lowest tricks
        Of any trade
My partner worked at BevHills selling crystal and china
        By the overpriced batch
One day he came home and told me about this chick   Who
        Was one walking talking juiced-up Snatch
Soon I was introduced to LUCY JADE   No woman born
        Of woman was more of a cartoon
She would mix Bailey's Irish Cream with Kool Wip Lap it

down

        And then proceed to eat the spoon
Sold crystal along with Junior   Filtching for herself all
        The nicest bits
Smuggled Lalique champagne stems outta there
        Between her big fat German tits
Rended a dead chicken between us Of all stars the one
        She did not resemble was Twiggy
Of any characters on earth she was a human replica
        Of fat Miss Piggy
Produced six plays with her playing leads or featured parts
All she ever cared about was how she looked or how
        She might break some fat-worshipping hearts
First time she grossed me out was when she visited
        My corporate office in Burbank
She squatted to pee in the incline of the garage Looking
        For all the world like a dressed-up Sherman tank
She tried to make every invert in every play I produced
        Regardless of the fact they were all fags
In the course of six years she established herself as one
        Of the most repellent homo hags
She would plop to her fat knees and give head Her
        Gobbling throat scarcely pausing to swallow
Hers was a life of promises Fat as her physique

Narrow as her intellect was hollow
Finally in the last project we did   She distinguished herself
        Giving head to a skinny dyke and a faggot with nerve
Positioning herself like a fat blob between them
        Cooing, *"Ahhhhhhhh guys! I live to serve!"*
After that we sort of abandoned her   knowing whatever
        She had to offer had already been nailed
And knowing without a doubt   She was the sorry aftermath
        Of the Summer of Love   The reason the
Counterculture
        Fucking failed

So: Lucy Jade, vanish into the night   Blithely unmindful
        Of what is up or what is what
Desperately trying to find pantyhose to fit you
        And trying to disguise the appalling smell of your
twat

NATIONALISM
AND THE RISE OF NATION STATES

New Nation States are rising from the muck
Of international turmoil and indifference
Out of situations which roil and suck
And stick their patrons with bad luck and stiff rents
Now we have Kosovo rising in the East
Dimpled semi Albanian Princess of the Balkans
But Jesus   Those Kosovars can be stunning beasts
With Big Chests   Big dicks   and callipyginous small cans
Further East, Russians are championing Trans-Dniester
Where the guys are uniformly Romanian
They have black fur outlining each and every keister
And say they're not as Turkish as the least Albanian
Russians are determined to block Kosovo
Having their own problems with Trans-Dniester and Abkhazia
Anyone who'd turn down a Transdniestrian stud is a schmo
And the shoulders on an Abkhazian hunk could not be snazzia
Further west both Frenchmen and Spaniards fear the rise
Of bourgeoning sexgods known as Basques
They eye French and Spanish bungholes as their natural prize
And seldom offer up their own tight furry asques
Off the west coast of Italy there's a land
Known far and wide as fair Sardinia
To our dimpled butts they'll give a helping hand
And then pretend they've never even seenya
Then there's the mini-Korea known as Cyprus
Stud Turks at tooth and nail with hairy Greeks
They g-string their hairy butts with cotton dy-press
Doublefuck in tandem
                Submissive British Geeks
Yes Boys   You all must understand
This surge of Nation States and Nationalism
Each new Race of Men features appetites
        Both strange and grand
New strange joys

New strange juice
   And New strange jissom

GREAZY CHOLO COCKROACHES

Oh what fun
Zipping down Hollywood Boulevard
First Spring rain pitterpattering softly
On the windshield of Jeff's Cadillac
We are the Lords of the Earth
We finally know how to Live
    Suddenly

Out of a fastfood parkinglot on our right
A Greazy Cholo smoking a roach as big as his dick
Driving a beatup Mercedes   Which he
       Probably stole or had stolen for him
Cut us off from the right endangering life & limb
Cocksucking sonofabitch
    I was furious

As we passed him on the left
       Threw him the bird
drove this bastard of a Greazy Cholo
       to further extremes
Of Cholo fury Could see his evil little brown eyes
Go into Kill Mode
For the next four miles
    Down Hollywood

Out Sunset through Silverlake to Echo Park
miserable little dopesmokin bastard
Dogged us thru traffic screaming imprecations
This sleazy cockroach *Don't need no stinkin badges*
Anyone who doesn't get this instantly recognizeable
       Film reference
Deserves to be hung out to dry
       For being cinematically dumb
    Anyway

His tiny Cholo fury finally possessed him
Went roaring over the curb right after the old
        Bowling alley
In Echo Park   Maybe he was going down
To Aimee Semple MacPherson's old Angelus Temple
To testify for his sins   worst fucking driver
In all of Los Angeles
Except for Korean housewives
Japanese princesses who drive Mercedes
        And BMGs
Their husbands have bought as guilt payoffs
For the Cholo mistresses they keep on the East Side
THEY are the worst drivers in Los Angeles
        Bar none

No wonder I consistently take the Metro and forget
        I ever knew how to drive a car

GUINEAS PULLING THEIR PUDS

If there is something better than baked beef and spuds
    It's full grown male Guineas
    pulling their poky puds
Now in the sovereign republic known as Italia
There's a new law forbidding the groping of genitalia
So an Italian stud wandering the streets of Venice
    Can no longer be a pud-stroking
    cum-oozing menace
He must refrain from pushing that particular sexual spark
Till he gets his buttboy secured
        Off the street and in the dark
I myself lived in the very Italian streets of downtown New York
Where the very air reeked
        of Guinea pud-pulling
        And the oozing of male pork
God forbid one should attend one of their entertainments
        Known as Festas
These hairy pud pullers always walked around grabbing ass
        Really jaw-dropping sexual arrestas
More than once a furry buttquesting Neopolitano
Would pull me into his clutches
        Seeking a *mano a mano*
So all I can tell Italian lawmakers   Trying in vain
        To push the unattainable a few notches
It's impossible to stop full grown Italian males
        From grabbing their crotches

DO WHAT I WANT

Do what I want you to do
Darling
Do what I want you to do
Just undo this thing here
 And take the next zinger
 And I won't malinger or screw
Just chew off a small bit of this
Don't mistake a deep buss for a bris
Please stop all this stalling
 It's really appalling
 For balling has led us to **this.**

 Once a boy
 Walked too carefully down the highroad of life
 Without once being asked to come out and play
 Yes: this boy
 Was never once considered as a husband
  Or a wife
 And he hasn't been to this day
 For this boy
 Is so damn careful he is calcified
 And there's no friction left in his fucks
 Poor sad boy
 Been so demented he almost died
 And what more can I say? I say:
  Shucks

Do what I insist you must do
 Sweetie
What I absolutely insist you must do
Let's go stumbling shackward
 And please don't be backward
All this cluelessness must have a clue
So let's solemnize this last tryst
Put a sound where you once might have pissed

And after that sound space
Let's get into this round space
And do all of the things you have missed!

Now this man
Puts one foot carefully in front of the other
Afraid if being balled
       Makes him being bossed
This poor man
Humiliated by his father
       Castrated by his mother
With his fingers and toes and his balls
       Very crossed
So with my proposal I'll apply this prospectal
While your pink little pecs
       Get all rosy and pectal
So let flow all your juices
And make mock of your Muses
And let's get embarrassingly rectal!

So do what I want you to do
       Fucker
Do exactly what I want you to do
Stop playing the sap here
       And adjust this small strap here
*So take **this**   Tell the rest to so shoo*
Just pull in this part of your crotch
*And adjust **this** just one nifty notch*
Skip advice from your aunt
And just do what I want
       And what you dread in this bed?
       *I say: **watch.***

UNDER THE ROCKS

I walk around through life darning my socks
Shining my shoes   turning over rocks
Rocks which have been strewn
          In the pathway of my progression
Each rock revealing a new man
          And a new furry sex obsession

Imagine my surprise when turning over
          A flat ocean washed piece of Atlantic shale
Found hot Mr Martin that fur covered wonderful
          Nova Scotia fuckable male
Far from the space which countenances a hint
          Of imponderable sexual rejection
Informed Mr Martin he had given me a whopper
          Of an old-fashioned Kraut man erection
When I revealed I was planning to travel
          To Montreal to hump some obliging piece of fur
He cunningly informed me, *"Why not hump*
          This fur upholstered French Canadian – Sir?"

          So I darned my socks and I progressed
          To the next fur covered hunk on whom I obsessed
          And in my gut I yearned for all those men
          Whom I could ball over and over again
          Over and over and over again

Then pursuing the rocks which strew
          The primrose path
Found hot Quincy now determined to bath
In mansperm I'm disposed to spew
          In   On   and about him
In my personal lexicon of sex
          I fucking cannot do without him!
In forbidding corridors of touchable tops
          Full of blind alleys and unaccountable twists

Told Quincy I was prepared to pop his cork
    With my two foldable ever-seeking fists

So I folded my fist and I progressed
To the next bottomfister for whom I obsessed
And my cojones cried out for all those men
Whom I could fist over and over again
Over and over and over again

Manpillow in Fort Meyers is another piece
    Of sexy fuckable manly trash
I'll fill him full of Krautsperm then toke up
    My special South-of-Panama stash
While we're floating on Pure Colombian
    Like all the best fuckable Florida men
I'll turn his furry body over and fuck that trash
    Again and again and (whatever) again

So I pumped my penis and I progressed
To the next sweet hole for which I obsessed
And my worn-out penis cried for all those men
Whom I could fuck over and over again
Over and over and over again

Hispalad in Southern Spain possesses
    The most delightful sportive tool
He has fled the Northern climes of wintry sports
    grim grey icy Liverpool
When we meet at Tenerife that Islas dos Canarias
    Sunwashed man dotted ocean rock
I'll stay on my knees for five hot days
    Sucking that fat juicy Spanish cock

So I plundered my tonsils and I progressed
To the next hard cock for which I obsessed
And my plundered tonsils cried for all those men
Whom I could suck over and over again

Over and over and over again

Arabmuscled in the District is a true blue sight
      For body oriented man-balling studs
Love to see that fur upholstered boy rising
      From a bath of herbs and beerpiss suds
When I've mastered all the ways to severally conquer
      This hot ethnically sexy slut
How many of those ways might involve
      His jaw-dropping dick-clenching Arab butt

    So I spread his buttcheeks and I progressed
    To the next furry butthole for which I obsessed
    And my butt-spearing penis cried for all those men
    Whom I could fuck over and over again
    Over and over and over again

    Yes
    Many are the rocks I've overturned
        And under those rocks
    Found good-natured, bad-natured
        And denatured men
    And when I've unzipped and undone myself
    I'm ready to turn over some more new rocks
    And after that some more new rocks
    Shining my shoes   Darning my socks
    Ready to turn over some more new rocks
    Over and over and over again!

DINOSAUR FOR LIFE

Wow John
You sure have united your recalcitrant party
Eschewing liberals   Gays   or anything arty
Stepping beyond Huckabee with his feet in the muck
To troll your Old Man Charm and keep pressing your luck
Rolled into the Casa Blanca   NRA credentials
    At the ready
Proving to Junior your shooting hand was more than
    Steady
Bestowing on the bastard one last insincere kiss
Knowing you are all there is between the Party
    And the Abyss

Strong John McCain carrying this heavy load
Eyes grim and steely   Neck swelling like
    A toad
Toeing a sandy line in the desert of Iraq
Threatening to bring Universal Draft on back
When that happens the Cholos and Rednecks
    Who abound you
Are going to put some nice hot tar and feathers
    Around you
With your dead ahead credentials and your skinny
    Trophy wife
The GOP shall anoint you DINOSAUR FOR LIFE

You vanquished Mitt and his smarmy Mormon brood
Vanquished Rudy   A monster straight out of *Edwin Drood*
Kicked some redneck mud into Huckabee's face
Pounded Fred Thompson right into fifth place
You've got the Old Man vote and you're stuck in our craw
But it seems you've failed to please rabid Rush Limbaugh
You're running on your rims   Fighting the Good Fight
But you're not shitkicker enough for the Far Far Right

So play us the Fear Card and keep us in tears
Keep us in the Middle East for the next hundred years
Keep all of our sons and daughters' noses in the sand
Build that spite fence along the Rio Grande
You know you can whip Hillary but Obama has you reeling
So keep retching up more of that Grand Old Man feeling
And when you spit your sputum in our direction
We know you'll never have another pertinent erection
So focus on Obama   Keep plunging in the knife
History will know you as DINOSAUR FOR LIFE

EGG ON MY FACE

I have drunk the deep draught of hemlock
My watch stuck at a quarter past five
I have darned the heel of the wrong damned sock
I'm checking my pulse to make sure I'm alive
My complexion needs serious assistance
There's no measuring my depth of disgrace
I'm the lowest of the low in the low low rents
And I have egg on my face

My fingertips are covered with hangnails
I got caught by my last bouncing check
If I were drunk I'd be sloshed in my sails
The red dye stops just short of the back of my neck
My most expensive pants no longer fit me
My character is surely unchaste
I'm covered with bites from the last man who bit me
I've an unsightly bulge at my waist
I'm tepid and terribly tired
I'm doubtful   Saturated with dread
My last tab of Cialis must have misfired
Since I'm now giving terrible head

My breakfast is purely bucolic
The cat got away with my kipper
I'm afraid I can't manage the next fucked-up frolic
Since my scrotum is caught in my zipper
I'm caught unawares in each caper
Something sticky ran all down my leg
And next to the toilet there is no longer paper
While my face is still covered with egg

SELL-BY DATE

Some of us have reached our sell-by date
This dubious bag of goods has been
      Too long on the shelf
Pawed over by legions of satiated
      Customers
With the barcode stamped on our asses:
      Much preferred by myself
We have been passed out as favors
      In daisychains and clusterfucks
As taste testers just before the choicest course
Been manhandled by four generations
      Of clutterbucks
All hoping to tap the mainspring of sperm
      At its source

Our own sell-by date I fear was passed
      Back in the eighties
 Been lingering too long in the Vale
of tales told and untold
Bitten by Mosquito Men   sucked dry
      By mules and maties
Kicked into categories: *too bulky;*
      Too hungry; too old
Watch my waist with the horror of one
      Who was always too thin
Pretending vainly that it doesn't matter or
      That I don't care
Knowing I have been relegated to the "Past
      The Sell-By date" recycle bin
Along with every other old beefed-up
      Furrybear

But *damn* the mystery of firm endowment
      I can still display
My shoulders and my chest are better

Than most of my brothers
I can compare my manhood inch by inch
      With Body Parts men any day
Knowing I will Tear and Compare as well
      As all the others
My butt has never known the opprobrium
      Of jadedness
My dick has often been compared with
      The very best
If my male beauty now falls into the sphere
      Of fadedness
I'll just tell you: *take what's offered*
      And fuck all the rest

So if you're shopping for a hot Competer
Someone who has the chops to share your fate
I'll administer a Fleets   Dare you
      To find a chap who's fleeter
And offer *everything* before my Sell-By date

VOODOO LOUNGE

In the Voodoo Lounge with my back against the wall
All round the room they are vying to mate
Pulling out appendages both large and small
Some one just threw up in the bartender's plate
Never should hang out in these Pleasure Palaces
Never should eyeball the boys like such a glutton
Now I have calluses on what used to be my calluses
Never should have unbuttoned
        That very last button

Here is Mr Sam fresh outta Fort Lauderdale
Pulling up his trousers heading for the door
There is the Otter from North New Jersey
Getting them to go down on their knees on the floor
Somewhere across the room the Dreamer is waiting
Waiting for me to give him the whammy
Wondering what kind of wierded-out scene I am creating
Wondering whether he should have ever left Miami

> *And we pull pull pull for the opposite wall*
> *Finding Tony tossing cookies in the toilet stall*
> *And we weave to the left and we weave to the right*
> *Wading through the bodies left over from last night*
> *Lucy has her dildo from the Johnny Wadd era*
> *Acting like something out of Conrad's **Secret Sharer***
> *At three AM we pick up whomever we can scrounge*
> *Getting to hell out of the Voodoo Lounge*

Holding myself back   trying not to swish
As they rush me I try to deflect 'em
Here's the Fallen Seraph from Central Mich
With someone's fist planted firmly up his rectum
Here's handsome Josh looking stoned and remoter
Than Mark who just looks used and slightly grey
There's sexy Biker Jimmy who has not had his quota

And I am so whacked I am totally glace'

Carrie and her mother have been singing Irving Berlin
Treating Old Hollywood like it was a Sacred Cow
Giving dead Cole Porter another tired spin
And the dawn is coming up like thunder anyhow
Cher just came in in one of her frightwigs
Looking like yet another bat out of hell
 Desmond just came in in a cockring and
              Roller skates
Left behind some glitter and a very bad smell

> *And we pull for the Bad Spa in the middle of the night*
> *Moving the red hanky from the left to the right*
> *Making sure we have our cockrings and our wallets*
> *Clearing that after-dinner trick*
>   *Out of our gullets*
> *The Bad Spa is rockin' at a quarter past five*
> *I am all fucked-out   More dead than alive*
> *Jack is hung like a moose though he isn't very tall*
> *And Joe is going down behind the waterfall*

Voodoo Lounge only half a mile away
Invites us to come and play and play and play
Miss Lucy cries like she was very bereft
 I move my hanky back from the right to the left
At seven AM my dick is turning purple
From the amount of action we've had
              Since yesterday's dawn
I look like a cross between Peter Cushing
              And Miss Marple
And everyone wonders what the hell is going on

Another raw Sunday morning in rotgut Palm Springs

Another raw egg in last night's beer
In my bed is one of those thick hairy things
I mistook for a man when I was feeling kinda queer
He fingers his nuts which are bound with twine
Wondering if I've been keeping any kind of score
Before I know what's happening he's got his hand
      On Mine
And I wind up doing just what I did before

> *Oh it's Hell on Wheels in the Coachella Valley*
> *A space marked SPERM in Rand and McNally*
> *Your trick parks his Mini Cooper sideways in the garage*
> *And we all go cruising in Rancho Mirage*
> *Fallen Seraph is still draped over the leather broncho*
> *Spreading his butt cheeks with all ten fingers*
> *All six of us are getting progressively Drunko*
> *Savoring the smell of sperm which suspiciously lingers*
> *Dawn is coming up like thunder at CCBC*
> *There are no more Night Trippers left to scrounge*
> *Unless they count you and possibly me*
> *As we haul our asses back to the Voodoo Lounge*

OMELET PAN/TA-DOC

Up there in that very humid place
Straddling the River   Valley Village yclept
There is a man with a very pleasant face
And a condition to make one cry,   *Jesus Wept*
For beneath a normal heart in a very normal man
He has an apparatus very like an omelet pan
Which keeps him wound up like a walking talking clock
And makes his great heart go,   *Ta-doc, ta-doc*
On Tuesday this handsome piece of Valley stud
Made my penis do more than bloom and bud
He lay his pumped perfect body back in his sling
And let me do just about anything

> *Feel the clock run the man like a hammer*
> > *Ta-doc ta-doc*
> *Slung in his sling like his own private slammer*
> > *Ta-doc ta-doc*
> *Dispayed for me there like one of nature's prizes*
> *I watch from my seat as his thick penis rises*
> > *Ta-doc Oh! Ta-doc*

Lubed up his perfect ass with menthol lubricant
The kind that made my Parisian buddies rave and rant
Let my collapsed left hand drift into the rosy hole
Where of course I was determined to drive my pole
But the pull and the push of the fisting I was giving
Made me glad that myself and Josh were among the living
When by gravity and choice
> Before either of us could blink
He had sucked me deep into his manself
> Beyond the second sphinc

> *Feel the little lips of the Sphinc pull me like a magnet*
> *Pulling me inward Upward Upward again*
> *This hot man on Moorpark is more than a fag net*

He's a hot sexy giving Man among Men
As my knuckles graze the side of that Omelet Pan
All I want to do is give pleasure to this man
Almost fainting from a sense of shock
Feeling that great heart go, Ta-doc   Ta-doc

Now I'm pushing forward focusing intensely
At all the pleasure I can give so immensely
My lips wrap over his swollen cockhead
Giving me something else to concentrate on instead
As my forearm muscles flex inside his anus
I go down further and further on a prick
      Thick   plum red   and veinous
 I must admit I have the talent and the guts
To take deep inside my craw
      Both of his thick distended nuts

    So he came for me there in that dark room
        On Moorpark
        Ta-doc   Ta-doc
Fisting   Fucking and sucking till it was almost dark
Over and over I tried to treat him with everything I know
Pushing deeper inside of him
        Giving him a helluva sperm-churning blow
Knowing both of our desires and demands
        Have not begun to reach their peak
I'll come back again to fist and blow him
        This next week
Maybe I'll mount him with my heart tucked
        Inside my pride
To feel that bodacious prick pushed firmly
        Up into my inside
And as my heart soars when he bursts the seams
        Of my Gibraltar rock
I'll hear my own heart explode
        Ta-doc   Ta-doc

PIG

I'm a pig
Not one bit ashamed to admit it
If I have pubic hair in my craw
      I'll just hack it up and spit it
I read Proust and Faulkner by the hour
      In a literary shower
But after only so much effete intensity
I'm overcome by my own immensity
Run around asking to be measured for my boner
Because I'm not destined to be a loner

I'm a pig
One sight of male fur
      Underneath a Levi's T
And I got hot as any pig can be
I hang on every treasured word of B. Obama
But when I see a big piece in someone's shorts
      My id musters up a whammer
 I go blustering toward my goal
Without a thought for sensitivity or soul

I get hard as flint at the sight of butts
I'm especially incensed at the scent of nuts
I want to get a little sugar in my bowl
And you can hear me howl when I get a whiff
      Of hole
Get huge at the sight of tribal type tattoos
When forced to pick between two men
      I hate to choose
When placed between two flames I am
      The moth of them
I'd rather be a pig And manhandle
      Both of them

Out on the dance floor we perform a six legged

Triad of a dance
A man like Alec Baldwin makes me dribble
        In my pants
The smell of man stuff makes me twist and shift
Still have wet dreams about Montgomery Clift
Have not even a residual touch of class
Pie in the Sky escapes me   I only dream of
        The Perfect Ass
Dream of that handsome stud in Toronto
        With nuts like boulders
Dream of the hunk in Stuttgart with black hair
        Across his shoulders
Dream of the absurdly handsome Sicilian
        In Melbourne
And that left-bent hunk in Rio
        Really gives me a turn
When forced to choose between the long short
        And tall of them
Like the pig I am
        I simply offer myself up to all of them
And when the diffident man or two
        Brings me up short
I charge them like the Pig I am with one rejoinder
        SNORT

MA DAISY

He is Ma Daisy
His eyelashes sweep against Ma Cheeks
I mean the cheeks on Ma Hairy Face
Actually his eyelashes sweep against
      Those other cheeks
The cheeks in a much more private place

Ma Brolly Daisy
Feel the veins in his biceps pulsing when
He pushes 'gainst my nether portion
      Once again
He has no cynicism like WC Fields
We love the way his little Rosebud yields

Ma Handsome Daisy
And when he presses his perfect feet
      Against the straps in Grandpa's sling
The Male Syrup which issues from him
      Convinces me   We can achieve
      Most anything

Humpin Ma Daisy
Ma Bonny Daisy
And when we're out in some smart
      Lunching place
He'll lean across the table   and give me face
While the straights in that smart luncheonette
      Are shocked to see what gay men do
He'll act just like Julie Christie in *Shampoo*
Sinking beneath the checkered tablecloth
To demonstrate   As a cocksucker
      He's no sloth

I just lean back and with one quiver
      I deliver

A quaff of stuff that shoots right
        To his liver
'Cuz he's Ma Daisy
And he's no slouch at giving head
.... Is he, Fred?

Ma Bloomin Daisy
When I reach round his gympumped shoulders
        To embrace him
        I'm never tempted to efface him
The stubble where he's shaved those manly shoulders
Just turns me on like crazy
And I get humid 'bout Ma Daisy

So when we leave the fray
        Return to his coupe
I drop my shorts Expose my furry
        Unshaved butt for him
        Go into total rut for him
Curl up like a male cannonball
        My knees into my face
        I'm such a gay disgrace
And he presses in for a friendly rim
I'll always expect the likes of him
        To rise above his station
to pursue some new abomination

'Cause he's Ma Daisy
and as everyone can see
He's just a
        Balls-out
        Fly-unbuttoned sex monster
                Whose plumbing pushes till
                It falls out
        No-nonsensible
        Beyond comprehensible

Sperm-dripping
Ass-licking
Barebacking Pig like me
And we both agree
As time passes on
And the mutual lust is gone
We'll just smoothly yawn and say,
"That's done, Son."

But at present it's really neat
To be mutually so much in heat
So much in heat that when I'm merrily
Attempting to screw him
Our kisses make me feel like I'm falling
Falling falling
Falling falling
Falling right through him

Oh, Daisy! What's in store?
Give me some more

POINTING THE BONE

Back in the good old days when I was three
My mom pointed her dainty little finger at me
Shook it hard and shook it long
Giving me the fuzzy end of her song
She let me know I was such a little rat
Spoiled rotten, every kind of brat
I had taken advantage of all her kind persuasions
To trump my own ace on several occasions
So to add to my suddenly negative *éclat*
I fired back,
     Why don't you back off, Ma?
And refrain from picking up another stone
While you keep on pointing that fucking bone

This did not go down well for a number of reasons
Soon I became known as the Brat for All Seasons
I was just as bratty as bratty could be
And her family all kept pointing their bones at me
Some of 'em would freak
     Some of 'em would fume
They'd point their fucking bones as I entered the room
Even though I was too pretty to even mention
Their pointing bones would add some more attention
Soon I no longer felt welcome in any of their homes
Since they were all pointing their fucking bones

Then in the local school yard   in that far-away dawn
The Pointing-Bone Game just kept pulsing on
Teachers pointed their bones, said I acted too smart
When I accused them of teaching Kitsch not Art
And on the baseball diamond when my catching went wild
They accused me of being a little Sissy Child
Then the bullying rose to a deafening furor
My Alter Ego decided to settle *this* score
My lesbian aunt taught me to punch

Like the late Art Aragon
Soon I was breaking their brat noses just for fun
If they wanted this malaise to multiply and malinger
They had just better try pointing another fucking finger

So puberty hit and I felt just fine
And another bone rose to the occasion – Mine.
Soon I was pointing *that* in a number of places
Boning out bookkeeper's and trucker's faces
Just a little smooth boy with no knife to hone
Suddenly producing this great big bone
Then my height exploded by twos and threes
With that bone swingin' right on down to my knees
All those truckers thought I was a bit of terrific
Or perhaps one might say, *bonerific*

Then I learned from my cousin that in times of stress
We pack a little more and care a little less
Both of us packed into some of our public parks
Boning out the population from the lights
        To the darks
And even with the Darks   with their legendary
        Endowment
Steve and I just continued our bodacious plowment
So when we connected with a Little Him
        Or a Little Her
Pointing our bones became our *raison d'etre*

Time passed. We achieved the peak
        Of our majority
Soon both of us became the focus of
        Maddened Authority
Known as Sodomizing Steve and Delerious Dennis
We bone-pointers became our own peculiar menace
Churchifying Satraps tried to lay the Law down on us
Threatened to close off the whole fucking town on us
So we zipped up our flies and wrapped up our pelts

And took our bone-pointing someplace else

Now after a lifetime of Boner Congeniality
The bone that is pointing is one of Mortality
I'm grinding all my gall and my kidney stones
And see the Shadows pointing their fucking bones
I feel like such an old burned-out sap
With the Shadows proclaiming,
    Dennis, this is a Wrap
So I'm zipping past these Mortality classes
Telling the Shadows to shove their bones
      Up their bony asses
And before I split this fucking joint
They'll know they've dealt with a Pointer
      Who really knows how to Point!

BLEEPING

As a child of almost seven Mom was forced to say to me
Of the words one should never *ever* say, there are ultimately
       three
First of the Three , she asserted, absolutely is
The one for which you should subsititute something else called
      wiz
Next on the list (one you might have missed
      when spirits begin to droop)
One should not spit out the shrew called Number Two;
      instead, you spit out *poop.*
Then (she said, blushing) there's a *nasty* word of which you
      Dare not peep,
Instead of that *nasty* word, one perforce must mutter:
      Bleep

I knew of course Mom's quarry, for, with my blessed
      Infant luck
I'd heard many times (from her own mouth) that word
      Which rhymes with "duck".
In this tetchy frame of reference, a vow she herself could
      Never keep,
Instead of the cursed "Duck" word, she still chose to utter:
      "bleep".

So throughout my youngest ages as I fell prone to stress,
I found myself uttering   *"Wiz, Poop, and Bleep"* to sanction
      My duress
Then I discovered Grandma (with whom one must never
      Settle hash)
Had inveighed upon my mother to forestall my mouth
      Of trash.
So I Wizzed and Pooped and seldom Bleeped Like WC
      Fields of yore,
And the Wizzing and Pooping and Bleeping made me
      Angrier than before

So, with Ma and Grandma safely away, with my infant
     Kind of luck
I'd scarify my manners with a manly   *"Piss, Shit, Fuck!"*

Now the whole idea of *bleeping* was a matter of not having
     Let it
Overwhelm me; as Shirley Temple said to Gable:
     "You'll get what I got when I get it"
Then one day when I was twelve, I got it. All this reticence
     I'd been keeping
Fell prey to a frail with a muff for a tail; and quickly
     I was *bleeping.*
Now Savannah thought I was so good at this
     She alerted her older sister
And Delilah invited most of her pals; soon
     My whanger had a blister
While servicing this covey of cunning cooze
     I fell prey to a special whim
With Savannah and Delilah knees-up and spent,
     I serviced their brother Jim

So this *bleeping* was really about *something.* And,
     Without reverting to smut,
I found that the talent I had for pussy I *really*
     Had for butt.
Yes! A blowjob is just a blowjob; but to claim
     That fellatial throne,
It helps if the King who's administering the Thing
     Possesses a bone of his own.

Seven thousand events of *bleeping* later, there's
     No promise I'll fail to keep
While I submit to the worst of the seven thousand
     And first,
I'll exhaustedly mutter: *"Bleep!"*

NO TURN UNSTONED

I have left no turn unstoned
Slipped onto the subway without a token
My Knife is the kind that's forever Honed
The bread I ate has now been broken
And in the truest wisest Wise
The wisdom I wanted has always been proferred
Knelt down for most of the livelier guys
Took each *soupcon* of Spunk that was offered
Went to the Plate with the mightiest Bat
Struck out with the left-handed Pitcher
Dogged my Dogs   Mewed for each Cat
When it was Bitchin' I was the Bitcher
Drank that Draught to its foulest Dregs
Running my tongue around the flagon
I've thick blond hair on my seaworthy legs
I was the Caboose for the Wonderwagon
Went running around with my hair on fire
Of spouses I was the *Trunkenweib*
The Ashes of the Nineties fuelled my Pyre
Did scenes resembling Abu Ghraib
Sobbed my Surrender into the Night
Moaning *Tangerine* like Martha Tilton
Bit too deeply with my Underbite
Took all of Paris but stomped on Hilton
Went ten rounds with Art Aragon
Checking the delicious curve at his Prow
Cried on all the shoulders I could cry upon
Wondering *Who* and *When* and *How*
Got kind of wild with the Wildebeest
Wondering how long it would take to get boned
Became the entrée at my own damned Feast
Because I have left no Turn Unstoned

LIMASSOL

I dreamed I was stranded in hot dusty Limassol
Waiting for the Turks to raise the bar
Watching the hot Greek boy with his hot black eyes
Still oozing man sap where I left him
      In the back seat of his car
Waiting for the Turks to suddenly see me
Knowing *their* man sap would rise   Soon as they saw me
Itching to run my hands over their furry shoulders
Hoping they would take me aside
      Ram and raw me
Hoping they would force me to my knees
      In the dirt of Limassol
Taking one hot Turkish cock after another in my throat
Fancying myself another long thin blond
      Peter O'Toole
Finding Jose Ferrer among these savages
      Is quite remote
I just want to be *savaged, savaged, savaged, savaged*
Want to be thrown down unceremoniously
      Upon my back
Want to be like the Living Torso Paul Bowles
      Wrote about
Just a living anus carried around in a sack
 I will submit to the brave Turks of Limassol
I will endure their sputum and ingest their spunk
I will take thick flower-smelling herbal draughts
      Up my nostrils
We'll all snort baby powder pretending
      It is junk
The Greek boy and I will roll over and over
      And over and over on the floor
While the Turks come at us with thick pricks
      At full mast
Eventually the Greek boy and I will retire to his
      Beat-up Yugo

Agreeing, between feverchapped lips and raw
      Roughened throats
      It was all a blast
And I will reward the Hussbear of Limassol
Who makes me ejaculate to everything I see
 I will submit to this rough sun bronzed
      Fur bearing animal
Provided, of course   He will submit to me

And so the Greek and I
fuck, fuck, fuck, fuck, fuck
    In the raw red eye of the Sun
        Where hands and hearts and assholes meet
    And soon we will leave off fucking hairy Turks
    And take our chances on the sands of Crete

O LUCIFER

Why do you keep
Leading me down
      Down down down
Avenues I'd rather
Much rather
      Not tread?

Because My Boy
My red headed overage boy
My hard nippled hairy chested boy
You will never be satisfied

BUT LUCIFER
All I want is a little kindness
A little satisfaction
In my drab day-to-day
      To day to day to day
Existence

Cocksucker
What you want is Heat
What you want is man to man
      To man to man to man
Texture
Spunk
And variety

DAMN LUCIFER
I should be happy
I'm loved
I'm admired
      Damn am I admired
Why do I keep exploring
Those hidden crevices
Those dark alleyways

In search of What

Stupid man
What you need is a big bare cock
Pumped to the max
        Down your throat   Up your ass
And after that
You need another
        And another and another

O LUCIFER
YOU'RE KIDDING

O SILLY MAN
        YOU are the one who is kidding

PROFANE IDYLL

As I dream the sleep of the truly depraved
There is no profane idyll from which I've not saved
A scrap of memory from which to excite myself
So much I could turn round
      Take my balls in my mouth and bite myself
My idyll is of the rich and strong not the weak
      And vanilla
My idyll is of the kind of man called a Killer-Diller

He comes into a room and the first thing I see
Are his hot sex oriented eyes staring out at me
Then I know the first thing about me to tarnish my escutch
-eon is the rapidly expanding Miracle of Me
      at my crotch
then as he comes at me like a House on Fire
I want to disarrange one key item of his attire
What causes me to suck in my saliva
      And begin to gloat
Is the thick trace of man fur at his throat

Then as I begin to descend into the sexual gluts
I rip open his shirt
      And lavish my attention on the fur
      That decorates him from nape to nuts

Engorging myself on fur that erects itself
      In tufts and whorls and ripples
In all that fur I discover the mystery of his nipples
Which engorge themselves for me as I lick
      And suck and bite
Causing them to erect even further to my delight

Now my penis is fully erect   has started to leak
But my sexual excitement has barely begun to peak
I sink to my knees unzipping his fly with my perfect

Prussian teeth
Exposing the pink thick treasure with which his DNA
          Did him bequeath
I sink the pink head of it mightily into my throat
All the way into my chest
          Only inches from my heart
          That part of me the most remote

Now he's panting moaning begging for More of More
This sexual stud has no idea what's in store
I roll him back upon his furry shoulders to expose
          His balls
The steam begins to drip from all four walls
Of the room in which our profane idyll is taking place
As I cram his bull balls into my face

Then as the moaning continues I slap those balls
          Till he screams with pain
If he protests I slap those balls again
As the thick hairs progress into his buttcrack
          Beyond where I can see 'em
I cram my pig face into his perineum

Rocking him back and forth
          Forth and back it's understood
Glutting myself on the prostate core of his manhood
I jerk on his prick all distended red and veinous
And plunge my fool face into his hairy anus

*For now **we have only just begun** to enjoy the fruits*
          Of sex
***Just begun** to reach the space where things get complex*
My tonguefucking produces hot wet ejaculations
          From his anal chamber
I'll fuck him with my tongue in a way he'll always remember

And now as he is prepared to give me the ultimate prize

I'll shove my Hot Eight up his butt
  Looking him straight in the eyes
And as we both **shoot shoot shoot shoot shoot**
  Fulfilling all of this profanity
We will have fulfilled the divine male promise
  Which has escaped most of humanity

STRAINING FOR STOOL

Here
Straddling the Porcelain Pony so full of it
Straining to pass a simply adequate shit
I review the events of a long fruitful life
Blessed with several husbands
  But not a whiff of a wife
Straining for stool to pass the first
  Audacious blow
When Grandma told me there was no one
  Half as low
As I could be when I opted to mimic Gramps
Demented Mick audacity shooting out
  Of both my lamps
Then Gramps himself gave me a secondary
  Whack
When he called me *that little Kraut fag*
  Behind my back

Dad of course cramming the figurative
  Pole up my rectal orifice
Sensing I had no Alpha Male hang-ups to dismiss
Then when his Badge Toting older brother
  Knelt to kiss my butt
Told him and his brother to get out of their
  Collective Rut
When my demented Mom whacked me seven times
  Across the face
On the main floor of the Bon Marche causing
  Total rout and disgrace
Vowed I would never again be anyone else's fool
Be caught with my pants down *Anywhere*
  Anyhow Straining for stool

As my life morphed to New York to environs
  Way beneath the rose

Learned lingering on the pot encouraged
        A more beneficial pose
As I sat for hours in various subway stops on the
        BMT and IRT
Finding definitively what a collective thrill
        Puerto Rican and Italian cocks could be
So what my pot straddling effectively entailed
Is to wait for the proper moment   when some stud
        Wanted his nether parts impaled
When some hairy Momser caught my eye
        My extension would go *Tilt*
Before long in that IRT powder room   Some Mick
        Seed would be spilt

Now we know Guiliani should be drawn quartered
        And run out of town
For choosing the Puritan Way   Shutting all those
        Tearooms down
Even today in all male premises   where favors
        Sexual are traded
My straining-for-stool pose has in no way
        Become jaded
For as I sit   Licking my lips   Scoping out each
        Stud in each direction
I'm at crotch level waiting to serve   the next
        Big fat erection
Now you American Puritans   wanting to roll
        The clock back   and close the school
Can hear me complaining   Cursorially explaining
        And always straining   But not for stool

GOT THE SHIT TO SHOE LEVEL

Arianna Huffington blogged about me
    yesterday
Her blog called me a terrorist and said
    I should be liquidated
My partner and I are preparing to leave
    Sunny putrefied LA
Quantum leap after quantum leap
    Of everything we've hated
The Ahmanson Theater is producing
    Yet another outstanding failure
We yawned through three turgid hours
    Of *There Will Be Blood*
Placido Domingo is starring in one more
    Miserable *Zarzuela*
This trickle of putrefaction is becoming
    A flood
HBO cancelled our favorite series
    Deadwood
The Bravo Channel is now programming
    Shitty reality TV
John McCain's replacement parts are now
    Doing what his head would
We've got the shit to shoe level
    And we'll all have tea

Hillary is claiming Obama is just another
    elitist
Obama has shown us Hillary couldn't
    Be elected
McCain has screamed that they both
    Are weak cowtowing defeatists
All three of them are more craven
    Than I could have suspected
Lindsay Lohan's mother is cruising girls
    At the Pizza Kitchen

Drew Barrymore is all scrunched up
      Trying desperately to be profound
Sarah Jessica Parker has convinced us
      That everything is bitchin
Broadway has a sizzling musical version
      Of *Legally Blonde*
Most Americans still don't know
      Canada is Up There
The Fox Channel is pitchin dirt so fast
      That it rankles
Cameron Diaz is still tryin to comb that cum
      Load out of her hair
And the shit has risen from my pink toes
      To my ankles.

Time, as they say, is disgustingly catching
      Up with us
We have knelt at the trough with the Stygian
      Pig
Even worse animals have queued up to sup
      With us
In the face of all this crap   My extremities
      Get big
Yes; even at the Stygian Trough I suffer
      This enormity
Gazing left and right for co-evalites to
      Commingle
Man after man gazes fondly at my deformity
This sperm-shootin schlong is not shit on
      A shingle
I gaze at the political community   Distrusting
      Every man Jack of 'em
Knowing each *Yes, We Can!* Angel is
      Probably a dork
I would really like to pull the chain on
      The whole pack of 'em
The shit has risen to eye level

And we'll all eat pork.

IT WAS A BABY-POO

Fiftysomething years and (slurp) ago
Mommy lay on her bed of pain
      Rocking to and fro
Hoping to hatch the Devil Seed
      She'd extracted from my Dad
Raging and irreverent
This Seed was Heaven Sent
To make this raging man-hater
      Infinitely *glad.*

For in the scheme of things
The slipstream of things
Hatching a *Baby-Poo* is the one thing
      That's required
To keep these lousy bitches
From breaking out in itches
To become a bitchin' Mom before
      Their shelf life has expired!

    It was a Baby-Poo
    Strong and lean and firm of limb
    A fucking Baby-Poo
    Just male enough to be called a Him
    Making amenities
    Swearing obscenities
    At the Navy Mothers before he was even four
    Baby-Poo wasn't nice
    Frankly he stank on ice
    But I was a classic Baby
       Like Baby-Poos of yore!

So Mom and I got risin'
And it was not surprisin'
By the time I was that obscene Four
      She was splitting at the seams

Emaciated and bulemic
frankly schizophrenic
Mom got sent to the Funny Farm because her Babe
  Was not the Babe of all her dreams.

  I was a Baby-Poo
  A darling Baby-Poo
  With my curly red locks
  At six, sucking men's cocks
  Never flinching from the grit
    In which I would dig & delve
  Baby-Poo exquisite
  And, some would say, "What is It?"
  Waiting for that fearsome penis
    To fuck truckers when I was twelve

Andrew Sullivan and his mate
  Were conservative to a fault
But somewhere at their Right-wing core
  They were what might be called Lacking
Andrew could dump Geo. Bush
  But what gave him the final push
Was an in-vitro smear of Baby-Poo so dear
  And the Miracle Babe who rose
  Sent Andrew's blogsite packing!

  It was a Baby-Poo
  Andrew and Mark said:
    "Ahhhhhhh. He's so White."
  No females 'round to screw
  Now this bristling Brit Bodybuilder
    Can fight the Family Fight
  So in his space entropic
  More than slightly myopic
  Andrew can set his Course
    Among the McCain-haters' slot
  Spreading his pelvis wide

Almost like Dracula's Bride
Because his Baby-Poo got cooked
In some rented lesbian's twat

Six Foot Two Sigourney Weaver
The embodiment of Beaver
Stomping the Hollywoods like some
  Valkyrie of old
Never enamored of Men
  Unless you count *Alien*
Over the pleas of horny guys
  She would continuously scold
Rather than feel a *bang*
  She consulted pal Chris Durang
From their old queer New York days
  They were continuously bonding
So in this way so queer
  They did an in-vitro smear
Now Sigourney has completed her Journey

  Cooking cookies and Clairol blonding

Sig had a Baby-Poo
A darling Baby-Poo
Lesbians from far and wide
  Came to spread the news
Chris never came up short
Shot in a glass retort
Now she can admire her faux daughters
  No penis and all cooze
Wonderful Baby-Poos
Marvellous Baby-Poos
Synthetic to the max
  Hoping to swell the groaning roster
They'll never drop the mask
And the result? Dare you ask?
  Sig barely paused to pass the flask

To Jodie Foster

AYE, AYE, CAP'N QUEEG

When our collective American chips are down
As nowadays they invariably are
We stand tiptoe in our Adidas
All dewy-eyed from near & far
And as the Captain of Our Fate
Stands beefy bilious and belligerent at the bow
We'll tell ourselves that he is Strong and Great
Wipe beads of sweat from each time-tunneled brow

> *Aye Aye, Cap'n Queeg! Graduate of the Hanoi Hilt*
> *You've brought the Oldsters on the Freedom Bus*
> *You've stitched VIETNAM on our Iraqi quilt*
> *Let firm fingers adjust and fluff your truss*
> *You've contracted us to another Hundred Years*
> *On the Playing Fields of Baghdad   Your own brand*
> > *Of squash or rugger*
> *You've hyped our paranoia; distilled all our fears*
> > *presented all of Islam as just another Bugger*

Cap'n, my Cap'n, give us peace from Liberals
From Him and Her and most exponentially, *Them*
You've pounded hatred of *Them* into all our skulls
Surrounded GOPodia with your fearsome phlegm
And while you roll and chuckle while you roll
Finding sinecures in Selma -- pill-popping dextrose
We all blush to find John McCain so droll
Sigh for a sight of manly leg – replete with varicose

> *Aye Aye, Cap'n Queeg! You can be our latest Ronnie*
> *While Nancy sends you Love Eyes of purest Moon*
> *You incant dreams of an America so sunny*
> *As it more and more resembles the environment*
> > *Of "Dune"*
> *We've fainted at the thought of these Pariah Preachers*
> *Pulsated at the places What's-His-Name might frequent*

And while we roar and ramble in the bleachers
We realize you've given up the Truth for Lent
But what's another falsehood between all us Cap'n-fanciers?
As you build yourself up to belch another overload
Watch as you prance like sundry other pranciers
Watch with bated breath. Since we expect you to explode.

I GET THE GRAVY

Preparing for Palm Springs, April 2008

In the hot-cookin' kitchen of my dreams
There are men cooking men. And so it seems
These men are forward and straight-ahead
Some of them resemble lumps of bread
As I watch them grow each studly beast
Is leavened with the manliest kind of yeast
These pumped-up, hairy sweetie pie men
Have yeast - dripping penii. And then
As my kitchen draws them up to completion
Each of them is a pop-up
       To the point of excretion
I watch those buns as they swell and swell
Which makes my sexual significants *kvell*
For here there is no *yes, no or maybe*
When the meat is baked
       I get the gravy

I get the gravy when it's nice and hot
Their gravy gets stirred in my collective pot
Re-heated with succulents and then
It gets thrown back into the pot again
And though some of these hearties might tend
       To get rough
They will still be spurting that gravy stuff
And we roll, roll, roll through the day and the night
Rolling in gravy to our great delight
Sampling the meat as it swells and droops
And none of our boys are party poops
We just suck each other's necks and moan,
       Heyyyyyyyy baby
Gimme some more of that home-made gravy!

So once more I prepare to descend on the Springs

The Kitchen which cooks so many interesting things
Hot meat above and hot buns beneath
And please remember to refrain your teeth
From making bite marks in all this stuff
For as I've said
         These boys can get plenty ruff
While stirring this gravy with all of these
         Swell beaux
I might get some gravy up to my elbows
As a master chef, I tend to give *everything*
Which includes shooting gravy out of my sling
So come on, boys! Each stud of renown
Can just whip out his gravy boat
         And chow right down.

ALL THE THINGS I DID THAT WERE WRONG

Well then, first I was born which came too late
I was half German which *I was told* was great
Then the Irish half which confirmed me a brawler
A libertine, a rake, and a bottomcrawler
Drove Ma into the nuthouse by the time I was four
She came back when I was five   Damaged
   Ready for more
Surprised Dad with one of his studly Marine tops
Groveling around the cottage sucking up slops
Everywhere I went I was hounded and taunted
But I taunted them back ... which was more than
   They wanted

  Because I always come on way too strong
  Because I do all the things I know are wrong
  Because I do them so well it makes me seem bright
  Because I know how to pretend those wrong things
   Are right
  Because I ask for the whole fish instead of kipper
  Because I always have one hand on my zipper
  Because any fuckpig knows just what I have in store
  Because I'm rock hard before my pants hit the floor

Hit the streets of Everett Wash when I was twelve
In the wide world of truckers to dig and to delve
Laid myself out in the sleeping rig in the back of their semis
Let myself get ravished under cold Seattle skies
While the truckers humped me I got rain in my face
Then I started humping *them* – to put them in their place
They got used to the feel of this big Kraut piece
Soon those guys needed more than that
   For blessed surcease

  Because we'd get tanked on Thunderbirds and Ripples
  Because I spat cheap wine all over their nipples

Because I did the Man Thing   due north and due south
Because I kept it clean and only pissed in their mouth
Because I knew how to give blowjobs like a bad wet dream
Because I separated the whey from the cream
Because I swallowed the cream as soon as it came
Because I was always ten steps ahead of my own game

As the wrongs multiplied in quantum leaps
My paramours found out I was playing for keeps
Moved to New York   Bought a mustard plaster
Jumped in the sack with Alan Bates and Burt Lancaster
Made the rough guy scene on the Hudson docks
Tearing off their clothes   Sucking their cocks
Trying (and failing) to keep all of this clean
Visiting the clap clinic on West Seventeen
Then when all my life was a rockin' reelin' joy
Descended like a tent on the Blue Eyed Boy

Because I was questioning instead of questic
Because I suddenly needed to be domestic
Because for years I'd been behaving like a dork
Because I couldn't resist that ten inch pork
Because my nerves were constantly twitchin'
Because I got tired of the group gropes
At the Broadway Central Kitchen
When I stood up straight I still looked stooped
And because I was suddenly always pooped

On the straightaway now toward 2010
Thinking sadly of what I do now
And what I did then
Thinking of that proud Kraut cock that never flagged
And those downy Irish butt cheeks which never sagged
When the red hair was real and I jumped all the locals
When I could see across a crowded room without bifocals
But still I know difference between a 'wrong' and a 'right'
And I can still get off fifteen times a night

Because I get depressed by all of these brutes
Because I get vertigo in my four inch boots
Because I refuse to eat rabbit and never frog
Because my ass looks perky
          In downward-facing-dog
Because I am determined not to be put on the shelf
And because
          I don't give a shit if I embarrass myself

FAR BITHYNIA

On the road to Far Bithynia, on a notable digression
I met a Lonesome Cowboy in the middle of the strand
His fine blue eyes were dimmed with the most painful expression
As he claimed to have the Map of Life in one big hairy hand

His shoulders bowed and humpbacked from his constant flagellation
His handsome mouth a twisted grimace of complete disdain
Because he claimed to represent the entire
      American Sick Nation
He stood astride the Path of Honor where none might tread again

I asked the Lonesome Cowboy why he'd sung his Last Hurrah
What caused his handsome flanks to lean
      And his handsome chest to wither
I wondered how he came to flaunt such personal *chutzpah*
He said, *"If I can't be the stud of the world*
      Nobody else can, either!"

    The road to Bithynia is long and to some it can be tragic
    Alarming or deforming or presage of certain death
    But this about our Cowboy was like sympathetic magic:
    The sicker he became it was like he was short of breath
    He ranted 'bout Republicans and some about the Other
    He ranted and he raved until he set us panting
    He bitched about the hapless broad who once
        He called his mother
    He ranted and he roared for the very sake of ranting

So the Cowboy disappeared into Frances Farmer Land
The friendship we might once have had I sensed we never could
His edifice of life became another frail Grandstand
And those of us who reached for him
      Got blistered if we would

As my own Rolling Coach neared Bithynia's fair towers

I saw the Cowboy and his Chariot stuck in a muddy rut
His visage flushed beet red (though he reeked of golden showers)
And he displayed his Manly Thumb
    Six fine inches up his butt

    Then I rolled my coach right on past the towers of Bithyn'
    As all the sheep knelt to worship the Lonesome Boy of Cow
    Shot back over my shoulder one devastating grin
    And wondered right out loud,
        "What's the point of this shit, anyhow?"
    So they all display their wounds caked with dirt
        Alive with maggots
    As Bithynia is turned into one massive columbarium
    And where they might once have been fine men
        They're a bunch of freaked-out faggots
While the signage outside reads:
    Lion's View Sanitarium

THE MADWOMAN OF SECOND AVENUE

The Madwoman of Second Avenue surveyed the room
Into which all her mahogany furniture had been crammed
She made a desultory pass around with a broom
Toted up all the ways her life had been scammed
Scammed by a thoughtless boy who just waltzed off
Leaving his family and friends behind him
And though the Madwoman had fumed and scoffed
She busted her butt to seek him out and find him
Scammed by Husband Number One with his wooden leg
Doing his fucking cheap Robert Newton imitation
Scammed by Number Two (a spectacular dreg)
Who used the Madwoman to elevate his station

Then came all the productive Working Years
With long-haired Number Three   Scrounging
        the Marketplace
Throwing a Block and Tackle on all those little queers
Painting that Annie Lenox look on her face
And then Disaster … Ah! Disaster! When her body revolted
Her spectacular outsides could not sustain
        When her insides were punk
She walked and she ran then she just plain bolted
Went to Ho Chi Minh City
        And got spectacularly drunk

She watched while her cats got thin and nervous
And Number Three played grabass with all the Expats
She got scammed to the bone for this expatriate service
Then she got more nervous than any of her cats
She returned to the States
        Shut herself up in a room
Cooked marmalade and made hot cross buns
Kept making desultory passes with that broom
Had scintillating visits from closet lesbians

But the poor Madwoman never knew what hit her
Or what the source of her irritation was
Left without a shred of gold or of glitter
She was just fucking pissed off because
She was just tired out from fucking Seattle
Because she had cut her hair a little too short
Because her nodded-out noggin had begun to rattle
And she was suddenly at a loss for a smart retort
Because she had truly begun to examine
That dark dank closet where
   The Grapes of Wrath are stored
Because she was just dog tired
   Of that damned smoked salmon
But most of all because she was bored

So she started to draw a bunch of little cute critters
Confronting celebrities like Michael Jordan and Cher
But nothing she drew could dissipate her jitters
Or the dissipating situation which had put her there
So she drew her mahogany chair up next to the oven
Ate one last hot cross bun
   To cushion her pride
Shucked of all this scamming those dudes had been shovin'
She tried a little Liane D'Exelmans suicide
Just enough quasi death to cause concern
Like Eva Gabor in that old picture *Gigi*
She put all those men and those bitches on BURN
And when she had made all the rest of us queasy
She rose up again Pulled her head out of the abyss
Because she was not a loser but totally bugs
She threw us all a desultory kiss
Because, let's face it, Fellas:
   The lady needs drugs.

SHE PUT THE LITTLE FUCKER
IN THE FREEZER

Liesl Schreck at twenty-two had three children
      Of both sexes
Liesl and her husband Franck moved from
      Slurbs to multiplexes
As their fortunes waxed euphoric   Liesl behaved
      More sophomoric
And Franck's *schlong* waxed upward too
      To get another baby was the thing to do

Liesl got fat and the babe grew fatter
      Liesl's tum forgot to be flatter
While her pregnancy advanced
      Liesl stopped being entranced
As her ninth month came into sight
      Liesl was experiencing Mama Plight
Finally, the kid grew upset with this spin
      with being enraged and still within
So, charged on Life and interior diesel
      The Kid popped out of Mama Liesl

    But she put the Little Fucker in the freezer
    She wrapped him in wax paper and interred him
    She rubbed the living babe down with the best fresh butter
    Then slapped him on ice – the way she preferred him
    And as his cries diminished – and the lid went SLAM
    She turned to Hubby Franck and said,
        "Get cookin', Sam --
    For nothin' spells lovin' like somethin' in my oven
    The Little Squeeze we can freeze with the pizza and the
ham"

Then Liesl made a point of being Mommy
Treated her big kids like she was Mother Teresa
She cuddled 'em in her arms

Displaying all her Mommy Charms
And forgot about the sucker deep down in the freezer
Then on Christmas Franck got a little too excited
Drank his Lieberfraumilch down to the dregs
He figured out just how
      To pork his little Lieberfrau
And put another sucker right between her legs

    But she put this second Sucker in the freezer
    The minute she went into parturition
    So another Baby Jerky got put down next
        To the turkey
    Wrapped in tinfoil; in a dignified position
    Two little babes slumbered on beneath the ice
        And you may feel now that Miss Liesl wasn't nice
    But her three grown kids were just too much to deal with
    Liesl had only just so much **weltschmerzkeit** *to feel with*

When Easter rolled around Franck once more
      Unsheathed his prize
Porked dear Liesl right beneath Westphalian skies
And, sure enough, soon as hot July was spinnin'
Liesl started to show she had somethin' in her *innern*
So she went full term with another brat and then
Wrapped the brat in phylo dough
      And slammed the lid again!

    She put a third Little Fucker in the freezer
    And just last week when the big kids looked for snacks
    They found Baby One and Two and when Baby Three
        Poked through
    They were shitting Prussian poop into their slacks
    So Miss Liesl got popped into the slammer
    For inventing a new form of Mommy Glam
    And what signified her worth
        Is that all her afterbirth
    Was wrapped right around a slice of Prussian ham.

NO MORE

No more abusive paranoia
No more rat's-ass diva attitude
No more half-hearted apologies
For acts that are *way* too rough and rude
No more bitches on their cellphones
Bitches of either dubious gender
No more bingedrinking saucehounds
On yet another alcoholic bender
No more of this spaced-out President
Claiming we are in the pink
No more hoity-toity musclequeens
Assuring me their shit doesn't stink
No more toothy smiling in my face
Then knifing in my unprotected back
No more collateral damage *anywhere*
        No more Iraq! No more Iraq!
No more of this Old Boy Entente
On Maryland's exclusive Eastern Shore
No more bloated senators who promise
Even more of what we had before
And as we watch the dollar sinking
Against even hard Canadian coin
We feel a tightening of the sphincter
And a loosening of our nether loin
We fear a brand new Cuckoo's Nest
With another meaner Ratched Nurse
And we know before it gets any better
It will have to get much much worse
We see testimonials on the Red Line
For another stupid Warner kiddie show
As the median age comes down to below puberty
And the things we know are so
        Are no longer so
So my pal and I drag ourselves off
        Into the distance

Beyond the lure of Tinsel City's call
We wonder why we endured this shit this long
Or why we ever put up with it at all
So I'm painting another coat of Verathane
On our beat-up old pinewood kitchen table
With a maximum of action and a minimum of pain
Just as long as we are physically able
And we see intrusive ads for *Speed Racer*
From our comfortable elitist perch
Comforted by the fact we can count the chest hairs
On furry delicious Emile Hirsch

PALM SPRINGS GOOD-BYE

Good-bye lovely boring flat Palm Springs
Good-bye Mary Bono Republican breeding ground
Too many promises   Too many once forbidden
        things
with the second mortgage going into turnaround
Good-bye to Debbie kissing women in cafes
        With plastic tables
Good-bye to this strange annex of Texas
        With stores called "Bea Dyke"
Good-bye to endless fur storage compounds
        Wintering minks and sables
In the heads of most you know for sure
        They still like Ike
Good-bye to annex communities with names
        Like Palm Desert and La Quinta
And the dreaded servant community called Indio
You cannot find a Democrat
        Or even a Democratic splinter
A revival of *Follies* is still the only place
        A theater starved boy can go
Good-bye to loosely organized Mongolian cluster
        Fucks
lubricated with mayo from the luncheon
        Table
Good-bye to all the seventysomething studs floating
        With their rubber ducks
Getting hard or semi hard whenever they are able
Good-bye to the frenzied Dinah Shore Golf Classic
Rememberance of days at once wilder and much freer
Good-bye to sunbronzed Dads who look
        much more Jurassic
Now all the energy they can summon is to slip on
        A cock ring and tilt a beer
Most of all good-bye to the forgotten "transit center"
        For the likes of us

Where the AMTRAKs are covered with blown sand
    From windmill towers
Where new nannies and maids from Baja wait
    forever for a bus
To be paid five bucks an hour to change Pampers
    And throw out the flowers
Good-bye, Jose Luis   Just another of many jerks
Good-bye Bill no matter how delightful your anus may
    Have proved for me
Good-bye to the towel men and the willing desk clerks
Much too eager to prove how their insides
    Might have moved for me
Good-bye, Good-bye lovely metropolitan Palm Springs
Carefully sequestered from life's bitter care and struggles
Can't help thinking things were better in the Forties
    With Cary Grant
Fighting off Randolph Scott and Charley Ruggles

HERE'S HOW IT WILL BE

Here's how it will be: red hot summer '09
Thirteen hot bear men scorching their pelts
I'll be done on both sides
      And inside … kinda fine
And they'll go … *"Lick, lick, lick …*
      Quick! Before it melts"
They'll perform solemn obsequies in a manner
      Quite nefarious
We'll all be *corrida* bulls
      Not one of us a steer
Some of us will fan our rectal chops
      In a way that seems hilarious
And we'll all be bisected as we're inspected
      From the rear

Hispalad will exhibit what he's fond of
      Exhibiting
Coop will be everyone's Unchained Melody
Otter of New Jersey will never be inhibiting
As he invites Kormoran to a dish
      Of cooling piss tea
Tanzbear will pass around his golden-bronze
      Prussian torso
While Keychain and Grecobear grovel
      On their knees
And we'll all watch out for Mr Universoso
As he cleverly elicits
      "A bit more of THAT, please…."

Creati41 will come straight out of Poland
Showing us what Polish cock can do
      For this mix
Cumgun will have shown us
      Sweden is not a slow land
Truthbear will have proved he's up

To all of our tricks
Sard2 will have opened up his perfect furry
        Backside
To all us backside-worshippers out there
        On the strand
And we'll pump like hell; at least there will be
        No slack side
As we leave our DNA on our bellies in
        The sand

Then the furry *mega-macher* from Belo Horizonte
Who gives the penis competition most of its heft
  Malepole with his featured member
        All erect and jaunty
And his big Brazilian penis slightly bent to the left
While the handsome grey haired man with the real
        Oral gift
Follows us with knee pads wherever we go
He will give our hearts a surge as he gives our cocks
        A lift
And we'll give him twelve different kinds of DNA
        To take back to Lake Oswego

This is already my dream   for an occasion
        One whole year away
Dreams can go up in smoke   in an incendiary
        Rush
So I'll prod, prod, prod with my cattle prod
        In my cheery way
And my aggressive stance. Which can only be
        Described as: *PUSH*
YES; pushing is what I do. Pulling is something
        Else I do
When I combine pushing and pulling not one of you
        Can scoff
We'll all be perpindicular   No matter what
        Else we do

As one by one, I greedily get all of you studs off!

DEATH OF A HUMMER

Mrs Doris Scyslinski age 44
Was the kind of conservative matron
      Barbara Bush might adore
She left none of her pals in the veritable lurch
When she dontated her services to the Evangelical Church
When she made sure the light bill was always paid
When she donated her last-year's playclothes to her maid
Letitia Hernandez a beaut of 32
Who was doing whatever she had to do
Boarding five buses she had to grab
To avoid being called a wage slave scab
Braving LA Metro and all those savage hard-ons
In the 25 mile ride from Hawaiian Gardens
To where she entered the pearly workaday gates
Of Loma Linda Road in Trousdale Estates.

Still Doris was not so remote a valkyrie
She might be distant from this plaintive query
When her husband Nick this very last summer
Inquired how many miles per gallon
      Doris was getting from the Hummer
Our heroine was never a one to shelve
A query this querulous. She replied:
      "Twelve".

Nick Scyslinski rose up like tortured Job of yore
Asked why Doris had not divulged this before
The Hummer was steamin' on its dashboard fore-guage
And the Scyslinskis were steamin' on their fourth
      House mortgage
They were no longer cutting the Schwarzenegger portion
And their teenage daughter Linda needed an abortion
So Nick, as ever the enterprising creature
Came up with the solution:
      Give the Hummer to Letetia.

So the Scyslinskis got a writeoff
        From the IRS
And Letetia had all her household saints to bless
Tooling the Hummer into the Gardens
        Like a good girl should
She was instantly the sensation of the neighborhood
Her teenage son Paco
        Yclept "Pacobell"
Soon had a score of hoary stories to tell
For as soon as his mother started snoring some Z's
He would tool the Hummer right down to the seas
In a neighborhood previously out of reach
He would cruise the hot chicks in smart Seal Beach.

But Pacobell's success was summarily dashed
When a rival Crips gang very dastardly crashed
Six of their vehicles with a deadly *thrummmmmmmm*
Right into the side of the venerable Hum
As a result of this tragic and very bum steer
Paco totaled his mom's vehicle right off of the pier
At Redondo Beach; and, sad to tell
Poor Paco totaled himself as well.

Doris Scyslinski took just one look
At the wreckage perpetrated by this teenage schnook
She totted up a score pushing three hundred thou
And without a look back at a "Why" or "How"
Had all the criticism of her church friends debunked
Paying for Paco's funeral
        And having the Hummer junked.

So Letetia crawls in her mourning dress
To the altar of *La Reina de los Angeles*
While Doris and Nick can cash this sacred cow
Writing off that total of three hundred thou
And in a gesture peripatetic or polyhedral

Doris donated sixty grand to the Crystal Cathedral!
Where, in the sunlight of the Just
  And the Born-Again
She can pray for the continuing health
  Of John (McBush) McCain.

COMFORTABLY OLD

Ahhhhh we dream of days gone by
     Johnny Ma' Man
When you were one hairychested
     Handsome Navy-boy hunk
Covered forehead to hoof with an
     Annapolis tan
Daring even one plebe to come within
     Three feet of your bunk
Those uncomfortable years
     In the Hanoi Hilton alone   Aloof
Practicing Conservative Superiority
     With your chastening glare
Emerging gloriously teeth flashing
     A stud to the hoof
With the look of the Immortals
     In your imperturbable stare

     But now you're Old Old Old Man Johnny
     Thirty-five years older than your boyish opponent
     Pretending you're The Man; pretending
          You're nothing like toxic and phony
     Logical successor to Team Bush; oldness posing
          As comfortable atonement

You came back to the States and you dumped
     Your first wife
You rose by the coattails of defeated Goldwater
In Sunbelt Arizona you spent most of your life
You married a beer heiress who looked more
     Like your daughter
You entered the Senate and rose plenty of gorge
Proclaiming loudly (sometimes shrieking) you're
     The Man with a Difference
But you got shaken out by the minions of George
Who claimed you got a Black Baby

On the wrong side of the fence

Now you're old, old, old Man John   standing
Firmly behind all your enemy's mistakes
      Even older than Ronnie when he rose
          To the Crown
      But you've stripped all your gears and lost
          Most of your brakes
      What you gained coming up you will lose
          Going down
      The hairy-chested stud of yore is gone
          like a breath
      Your seventysomething hulk draws you down
          Into sleep
      You totter into idolatry which is something
          Like death
      You're rocked in the cradle of the Dubious Deep

      So get into denial of the Young and the Raw
      And those who hate your war;
          And your tremors and strokes
      And stick your seventy-two soft years in our craw
      To be Comfortably Old doesn't mean
          You're Just Folks.

RALPH NADER STINKS ON ICE

Once we all had prehensile tails but they've been gone
    For ever so long
Once Stephen Foster was the musical rage but he's *verklepft*
    On wings of song
Once Bette Davis was a very young girl and everyone
    Thought she was nice
And once Ralph Nader was politically correct; but now
    He stinks on ice.

New Orleans was once the Queen of the River; but now
    She sinks in a swamp
Christie Alley could once make me twink like a mink;
    She's now three hundred pounds of rump
Speaking of minks, those deplorable thinks could never
    Be eaten with rice
And the way a mink thinks is all knotted in kinks
    Like the way Nader stinks on ice.

Our Afghanistan bases were once safe places and W
    Still lives in a bubble
A Guantanamo vet was once waterboard wet
    But they're all in terrible trouble
I once was in love with my looking glass but I'm
    Tired of my terrible self
But there's nothing muleskinned as the stinking wind
    When you get downwind of Ralph

Ralph Nader! Ralph Nader! What makes your arteries so hard
Dispensable Ralph Nader Just get back down in the yard
We once called you The Spoiler; and quaked in your presence
But now you're known as The Skunk
    With your putrified essence

So try to dump on Obama; he's more Teflon than Ronnie
*No, Ralph; you're just **old** and that's not even funny*

Your burrs attract curs and your flogger's not welting
And the ice on which you stink
    Is casually melting.

Let's forget about Ralph Nader   the Spoiler of Old
His spikes have turned to rubber;
    the rest has gone to mold
He's sinking like the Titanic in a veritable trice
And in case you've forgotten the fucker is rotten
    And he stinks to hell on ice.

LITTLE GIRLS

On the op-ed page of the *New York Times*
    Stocked on all the drugstore shelves
The cover story is about little girls
    Who have dolls dressed like themselves
They've missed the point; these darling girls
    Like their dolls from stern to stem
Are actually the *doppelgangers* of their dolls
    And designed to dress like *them.*

In days gone by (which I vaguely remember)
    We had Alan Ladd as a sailor
 Clark Gable as almost anything;
    Christopher Lee as Vlad the Impaler
We had Bill Holden with a hairy chest
    And Bill Holden shaved and without
We had Brian Donlevy with his tweakable tits
    As if there were any doubt
We had little Johnny Downs with his pouty look
    And Carleton Carptenter tall and fruity
And then James Dean whom our senses shook
    When any kook could be his cutie

But little girls had virtually no one; Shirley Temple
    Was declassee
Margaret O'Brien had risen and fallen again
And Doris had had her Day
Only Liz Taylor was the great Enchantress;
    For the legions of Barbed and boobed
Elizabeth taught us to love horses and chipmunks
Till Elizabeth (fortunately) pubed

Then suddenly from that little-girl form
With that squeaky little-girl voice
Exploded a pair of English knockers
Like the fenders on a frenched Rolls-Royce

No more the precious Little-Girl Liz
Like the flame on a zapped-up Ronson
Elizabeth became the carnal object
Of Robert Taylor and Van Johnson

Now in our suddenly Re-Puritan day
Little Darlings reign supreme
Disney is the flavor of the new decade
 Abby Breslin their new wet dream
But as John Huston told the little bitch
Who Columbia had selected to play Annie
"Dearest, you'd better learn how to suck
        a fat thick cock
Than to tempt dirty old men with your fanny".

Yes, Little Girls were meant to be fucked
And fucked and fucked again
Then on off days, they should be serially fucked
By even the grubbiest men
And on Mondays they should be fucked
And on Tuesdays they should be fucked
And on Wednesdays buggered and raped
On Thursdays they should just go back to putting out
        As the week is variously shaped
Then on Fridays they should go down on lesbians
As a way of shaping their craft
Saturdays they can put out
        For Liz Taylor's horse
And if they think they've gotten the shaft
We will promote them to executive positions
On the NASDAQ 100 and then
While they are laying down corporate clout
They can put out for all the men
Yes; Little Girls are always spoiled little brats
In the most remote of foreign lands
And they provide shocking amusement for
        Fags like me

Tittering behind our hairy hands

FACE SHOTS

Adventuring from site to site
From dyspeptic day to fractured night
I encounter penises of every size
From all kinds of horny priapic guys
I'm invited to inspect backsides of fleece
From the Gulf of Guinea to the Isles of Greece
And to put my face into every tush
Of descriptions rivalling Hieronymos Bosch
But what really floats my boat for me
Is the handsome visage which I might see
Accompanying the pricks and tushes and balls
Sending me over my private Niagara Falls
For the pricks and tushes and balls are drones
That do nothing for me without good cheekbones!

O handsome man   You have the earnest art
To light the fire in this erratic heart
Give me the mighty nose of some Sephardic Saracen
I'll rush into his cave
            And feast upon his barer skin
O handsome stud   My skin has lost its paleness
When I encounter your Mediterranean maleness
Accept my worship;
            Let's have no solemnities
And I'm content
            To discover your extremities!

So be prepared to put me to the test;
Dick shots are nice.   But face shots are the best!

FEAR ITSELF

Franklin Delano Roosevelt
The hawk faced man who served three terms
As President of this beknighted country
Three terms and then some   before he fell
    By the Georgia wayside
And Harry Truman took over

FDR said at the beginning of his first term
When half the banks of this country were in
        Default
The Dust Bowl was raging in the Midwest
Territorials in the Philippines were openly
        Revolting
And his wife Eleanor was having lesbian sex
        With a woman in the Army
He said: *the only thing to fear is fear itself.*

He was so right   good old FDR
His words still ring true today
It's what we need to hear when fearmongers
Stand outside our doors screaming their wares
We know there is so much more fear
        In store for us
All the rockribbed conservatives cringing
        In fear of what they know
Will change their comfortable lives forever

The entire Solid South cringing at the thought
Of an intelligent man whose skin just happens
        To be a pale coffee color
Whose mother was white as white could be
Being President of this ever beknighted country
They want to cling to the bull necked old
        Navy guy
Who looks like he's about to explode any minute

And does explode with regularity
      On the floor of the Senate

We are in fear of our own children
Whose savage rites we don't understand even
      The reason for them to exist
The rites that is not the children
We are in fear of our parents going down
      To impoverished death
In fear of the doctors who scrape our wallets dry
      Even at the spectre of the common cold
 Soccer Mom whose trusty Range Rover
      Took her handily from playschool
      To playing field finds herself shelling out
      Four hundred bucks a month to transport
      Those little suckers   Fear takes hold of her
      Right where the Tampax should be
      While she's standing at the gas pump

Still the Old Tigers whose approval soared to
      80+ percent after 9/11
When they all blew so hard most of us believed them
(But not this cat)
Still the Old Tigers show no sign of changing their
      Tactics
Ignoring global warming
Ignoring demands for living green
Ignoring the screams as Freddie Mac and Fannie Mae crash
Now we understand with horror they're using
      The good ol' CIA
Our all-purpose agent of terror and subversion
To create new nationalistic wars on the outer fringes
      Of Kurdistan and Baluchistan
Yeah those outer fringes touching Iran

Iran will be fighting a red hot war on two fronts
Funded and sustained by our tax dollars for those of you

Who are taxed
And Oh   our Advisers
Blackhawk and Halliburton will be right in there
        Setting up shop
No matter what a new Administration chooses to do
        Or tries to do
The die will be cast   We'll be in the soup
        All over the Middle East
None of our superheroes will be able to save us
Iron Man will just turn a deaf ear and do another line
Hancock will lie back in his sweats and grab some more
        of Charlize Theron
The Hulk will revert to being Ed Norton for good
        And go back to his bad old ways at the Fight Club
Christian Bale will forget where he put his flying suit
None of them
        Not one of them will be able to make us forget
        Our fear

And Oh
While all of this is going on more & more of us queers
        Will get married and raise cats
The anally retentive guys at Focus on the Family
        Will have conniption fits
Try to take it all away from us but it will be
        Too late
All of the old reasons for our fears have drifted
        Past their sell-by dates
All of us old unreconstructed Liberals will have
        Brand new fears

Like

How to behave when David Petraeus is acclaimed
        Emperor of the Western World
And civil liberties in this beknighted republic
        Are shut down forever

THE GIFT THAT KEEPS ON GIVING

The Gift That Keeps On Giving is my inimitable wit
Couched in the hidden fury of sarcasm
Guaranteed to slay every dumbassed no-nuts Twit
And push the crackbrained clod
       Into a Loser Spasm

The Gift That Keeps On Giving is my flair for romance
How many lucky men I can ask to be My Valentine
With the romance comes innumerable ants in my pants
And all the pangs and stings of things
       Which are inimitably Mine

That Damned Gift is wearing out its welcome
It's been dragged across too many dirty floors
My precious gift has become a hell-home
Not fit to see the light of day
       In the unsparing out-of-doors

My Gift which keeps (wearily) on giving is my perfervid brain
Always inventing new ways to stretch awareness
What I have done (well) before I will certainly do (well) again
Without an ounce of favor or, (occasionally) fairness

The Gift which keeps on (inexorably) giving is that
       Big piece of meat in my jock
Gifted to me by my (equally inexorable) Prussian DNA
This precious gift makes it possible
       For me to fuck around the clock
Gasping panting bottoms have no chance
       To ask me how I got That Way

So I will work that threadbare Wit   Do the dance
       Of insufferable Romance
Milk that feckless brain till it feels no pain
       Pack that Prussian meat into a pump

And if, my dear, you think This Package is way, way
        Too queer
I will simply ask you to take YOUR package off
        To the nearest city dump

        Because I'm Special;   Really a Piece of Work
        Because I'm the Kraut to whom few can hold a candle
        The man who blows me off is really some kind of Jerk
        I'm hard to hold and equally hard to handle
        My heart has been accused of being black;
                Sometimes I mount a Sneak Attack
        But during all this stress   I'm still damned glad I'm living
        And while I feel the Winds of Time
                Whistling up my Well-Used Crack
        We can all appreciate my being
                The Gift That Keeps On Giving!

THE THELMA & LOUISE MOMENT

It's finally come   The Thelma & Louise moment
Yeah finally after 31 years of living in LA
    And loathing it
He & I looked deep into each other's so-much-alike
    Pale blue eyes
And said   *Let's get the fuck outta here*

We are moving to Santa Barbara
A small city with history and quiet and real culture
    And quiet
And people with manners and quiet
And a conspicuous lack of young adults on skateboards
Wearing all-black and mouthing *awesome*
    As a response to everything
No teenagers on every corner cellphoning teenagers
    On the next corner
No crippling gridlock traffic in a traffic grid
    Where one out of every five cars is stolen

Los Angeles is a city suffering from giantism
When mentally it is still in Kindergarten
Allowing atrocious animated billboards 200 feet high
On unaffordable condo buildings which may never be built
Disgusted by our gladhanding wife-abusing loose cannon
    Of a mayor
Amused as all hell
Now that we're locked in a gas crisis   Jewish matrons
Who one year ago gleefully cellphoned from behind the wheels
Of their gas guzzling SUVs   Now rush about like fish out of water
In the trackless underground of the Red Line and the Purple Line
Frightened to be faced for the first time in their privileged lives
With People of Color other than maids who come in to clean

I work with the core voter registration team of the Democratic Party
Out on the fringes of the Gold Line in Pasadena

Registering people to vote who've never voted before
Registering Republicans who knelt at the feet of Rough Rider Ronnie
    As Democrats
Registering fifteen hundred people in one day between Sierra Madre
Villa
    And Chinatown
Always looking around   Looking around   Saying to myself
    This is the last time I will be doing this

The last time I'll have to hear the sports wonks
At that very good Szechwan restaurant in Chinatown
Getting their rocks off about some non-event at Dodger Stadium

The last time I'll have to listen to some hawk faced Former Soviet
Grandmother hang up the checkout line at Smart & Final
Over the issue of payment in pennies

The last time I'll have to watch fat bellied Nebraska moms
At Motel Six mingle with blue haired junkies and walk haplessly
Into the street   Wondering why the big black dominatrix
Across the street is carrying a whip

The last time I'll have to hold my breath going into the john
At Canter's because the night crowd has smeared feces
Over all the walls

The last time I'll have to hear brain dead young women
In their twenties beating each other up in the street
At 4:30 AM   Beating the shit out of each other in the middle
Of Franklin while traffic   That same unending traffic
Surges on about them

The last time I'll see a huge reproduction of Angelyne
Taking up the sky above Hollywood Boulevard

The last time I'll see Hollywood Boulevard

Fleeing fleeing fleeing this semi city with its semi culture
To which I had to be dragged kicking and screaming in the first place
Only because they were waving forty thousand a year in my hungry face
All the fruitless years we tried to buy into this crappy boob oriented
            Music and film culture
All of our great actors paying lip service to Significant Art
Then doing voiceovers for stupid animal movies
All the pumped-up young gay men with college degrees
Rushing to see the stupid animal movies

Sick of it   Sick of it Sick of it Sick of it

We are approaching the Thelma & Louise Moment
We will get into his Prius and drive silently to the old city
Way out there on the continental shelf
We will luxuriate in Endless Quiet
And return to Los Angeles only for Philharmonic dates
    And the occasional probing session of acupuncture
        Just to keep our plunging testosterone
        Tweaked

ARMY STRONG

Above the bus seat above my head
    And to the left
The US ARMY has a recruiting pitch
    Of calculated heft
US ARMY (ARMY STRONG) it sez:
    Then they dive into the trough
With a money laden pitch
    To jerk you poor dumb kids off

There's a $71K college fund   for those of you
    Who can actually read
And another $40K enlistment bonus
    For those of you in dire need
And all you patriotic redneck boys
    And physical education slags
Can count upon being airlifted to Afghanistan
    And shipped outta there in body bags

Or you will be cannon fodder for the two hot wars
    Bush & Co are planning in Iran
Our ever ready CIA is revving up anger and hate
    So they can rise up all Baluchistan
And for you geographically-challenged high school kids
    Batman Ironman and Spider-man nerds
The CIA is planning yet another red hot war
    To rise up all the Iranian Kurds

So three cheers for Captain Spaulding   the US ARMY
    Recruiter
With overwhelming whiffs of Groucho Marx
    Who never would have been this kind of shooter
But make sure to email Patrick.Spaulding@usarec.army.mil
    To let him know in no uncertain terms
    How this latest Army pitch gives you a thrill
And if you're *still* infused with McCain-driven testosterone

And hate   Like any normal kipper
Just use earplugs for predictable mortar fire
       …you won't need 'em for the ZIP of that last zipper

PRECIOUS THINGS I LOVE

I love to enter the dance floor in a tuxedo
    And wind up losing my fanciest pants
Love to start dancing with a beautiful woman
    Then commence groping the ass of a nance
Love to think of all the nasty things I know
    And put them all in this one little space
Love to hit the sack with four men
    And have them all (sequentially) sit on my face
Love to rub my face with the white of an egg
    Though nowadays the effort is all in vain
Love to get into a very conservative crowd
    Then say disgusting things about John McCain
You may never have heard a more encouraging word
    When I'm comforting a widow who's all bereft
Then I struggle into a loose pair of silk pants
    And let Junior do His pendulum from right to left
Love to get between a pair of high keyed gals
    So I can enjoy the excitement between Her and Her
Love to shag a really hairy old fella
    So I can lose my fingers up to the knuckles in his fur
Love to have adventure after dangerous adventure
    Because my alter ego dotes on adversity
Love just about anything by Woody Allen
    Because I enjoy his eternal perversity
Love to share a bong with a company of stone freaks
    Love to watch 'em get higher and higher
The only thing I loved about *Tropic Thunder*
    Is when Downey got down on Tobey McGuire
Love to play with a fresh split of champagne
    And cover all my putative lovers with fizz
Love to fib about my oh so elusive age
    And make you all wonder how old the fucker really is
Showed up at Ronald Reagan's funeral in Simi Valley
    Just to make sure the old cocker was dead
And of all the very Precious Things that I love

I love fucking a man's brains right through the top of his head
Because I'm such a good guy   Such a nice guy
    And the last image I'll leave you with before we retire
Is that I love to share all these Precious Things I love
    And …. Oh! Have I told you? I'm a great lover
    ….but I'm an even better liar

WE ARE ALL GEORGIANS

Yeah   The thick necked stump bodied presidential candidate
Stood as tall as he can stand   Being only five six and a bit
With tears in his rheumy eyes he cried out
                    "We are all Georgians!"
Then proceeded to whip it up   Delighting the miserable folk
In Eau Claire or Kenosha or whichever fucked-over rust belt town
He was campaigning
                    "We are all Georgians!"
Shit John
Till only a week ago most Americans thought there was a new
Political phenomenon going on down there north of Florida
South of the Carolines   But it is just the usual bullshit
                    "We are all Georgians!"

Goes hand in hand   Foot in mouth   With the other catchphrase
                    "Drill, baby, Drill!"

That poor sap Mikhail Shaakshivili   Poor dumbed out
Former buttboy for the American Enterprise Institute
Johnny-on-the-Spot in that cultural backwater Tiblisi
God how much America cares about the Sovereign Republic
            Of Georgia   Like hell

Condi and George and Gates greased the skids for Shaakshivili
Goaded him into being our White Knight
            Georgian Don Quixote charging the gates of the Evil Empire
Remember Saint Ronnie and the Evil Empire

Suddenly it's news South Ossetia   Abkhazia   Places most Americans
            Never in their lives have heard of
They have been de facto part of Russia for twenty years
Only the old artificial boundaryline set at the Versailles Conference
            Way back in '17
Determined South Ossetia would be Georgian
North Ossetia Russian   Omigod   All the oil rich Sultans

Of Russian Petrobusiness
Have had their summer dashas in Abkhazia for fifty years

Still
Mikhail Shaakshivili   Hoisted on his own petard   By our leaders
Like a fat cocktail sausage on a Korean frill toothpick
Charged South Ossetia with his antiquated army of mavericks
Hoping against hope Condi would come riding to the rescue in her
Hummer
      …but she never came

                      "We are all Georgians!"
Sure

As the plump little man rushes about waving his pudgy hands
Screeching

"Drill, baby, Drill! We are all Georgians!"

Yes we are all Georgians   We are all Georgians in the sense
That we have this endless appetite to be gulled by our fearless leaders
Who don't give jack shit about the Republic of Georgia
Other than its being a stick in the eye of Moscow

But it's a good distraction   While Iraq is totally fractured
Afghanistan ready to implode   Pakistan ready to go ballistic
We can go back to playing the Good Old Cold War Game
     Russia Fear

So get out there John and do your usual rant
While your skanky wife tries to keep the true profits of her beer
millions
       Out of the headlines
You guys in the national press have really given this pumped-up Navy
Brat
       A free ride

Bullshit

We are all lemmings headed for the cliff while Joe Lieberman
Skinny Sancho Panza from Connecticut
Keeps reminding John which countries are Sunni and which Shiite
Like any of those cocksuckers cared
Cheney never did   Rumsfeld never did
Condi knew but she pretended it didn't matter
Now they all go about screaming with their hair on fire

"We are all Georgians!"

I am not Georgian

I am one of 300 million disenfranchised Americans and I'm heading
For the bathroom to *fwow up*

Because too much of tiny Georgia just got stuck in my craw

THE GLOVES ARE OFF

"We are at War" intoned bull faced CIA director Tenet
Since We were at War that of course could justify
Anything   Repeat Anything   The CIA wanted to do
To purge our environment of our frightening enemies
To force Enemy Aliens to speak out against
        Other Enemy Aliens
The gloves were off   David Addington   Dick Cheney's
        Muscular bearded lieutenant
Advocated extreme forms of coercion   Especially torture
John Yoo   the right wing policy wonk from Pepperdine
Called the Geneva Conventions "quaint" which of course
Was picked up by the Bush Administration's professional parrot
        Alberto Gonzales

In early 2002 the CIA detained a Canadian citizen
        Maher Arar
As he left a business meeting in New Jersey
        On his way home to Toronto
He was led peacefully to a silver private airplane
Leased over and over again for extraordinary renditions
By a CIA subsidiary Jepperson   Which operates
        Out of a Boeing hangar in Everett Wash

Arar was taken first to Washington then to Bangor Maine
They fed him the best shish-kebabs and told him friendly stories
Then the plane went to Rome and to Amman Jordan
By this time Arar knew something pretty snaky was up
It landed in Damascus

Two weeks before Bush decided Syria was Number Three
        On the famous Axis of Evil
Evidently not evil enough not to be prized by the CIA
For the efficiency of their torture chambers

Arar entered the edifice known as Far-Falasin

Aka "The Grave"
He spent the next three years in a body slot
        No longer than his own forearm
There was a grid above where cats urinated on him
Slots across the floor made it possible for rats and roaches
                To roam across his feet
                So they could ingest the prized cat piss
Arar was forced for over a year to accommodate
                Larger and larger foreign objects up his ass
                Till it was bleeding 24 hours a day
He was hung from the ceiling and had electro shock cables
                Attached to his testicles
He had his shins whipped with two inch steel cables
                Till he was no longer able to stand
After three years of this he was capable of telling his
                Interrogators anything

He did

All the time his wife was trying frantically to have the
                Canadian government intercede
With the US State Department to no avail
State had been left out of the Torture Loop
                As prescribed by Addington

Finally in mid 2005 the Canadian Government forced Syria
                To release Arar
After he had "confessed" a mindless gobbledygook of
                "admittance" of terrorism
Canada paid Arar $10.5 million for his pains
While he is still listed as an Enemy Adversary
                By Justice and State

All of which was taken very seriously by State
Along with several other equally fictitious "confessions"
                Exacted by torture
Colin Powell went before the United Nations and made his

Blundering speech
Linking Al Qaeda to Saddam Hussein
All based on these lies and many others

Everything in our society as we know it is based on lies
People who've never served in the military direct our military strategy
People who have no background in law dictate our legal memoranda
People who have no more than a passing interest in government
        Govern us
People who think the Consititution is something to be pissed upon
        Like the cats on the grid
Teach classes in Constitutional Lew

We are the Worst of the Worst
And here we have a bull necked   cancer ridden old man
Who had been tortured for five years by the Vietcong
        Advocating torture
America is thrilled by these sadists and their bullyboy tactics

Unless of course
They are the ones who take the free shish-kebab flights
To Far-Falasin

I expect it to be my destination one of these days
When one of my casual email buddies
        Incensed by my left-wing rant
Decides to rat me out to the CIA

How many old crypto liberal fags can they stack up
On the filthy roach-ridden floor of Far-Falasin?

As many as our leaders like
In the name of patriotism and anti-terrorist necessity

The gloves are off

Yes

They are

SIMPLISTIC SARAH

It's SIMPLISTIC SARAH   tall and slim
    Very much a Her and not a Him
The new puddle of Moose Poop
    That Stupe John McCain has stepped in
She's as pretty as the Borden Cow
    Never wondering Where or How
    And she is ineluctably productively Vanilla
She's an ice hockey mom
    And she was queen of the prom
    In suburban disturbin'Alaska (Wasilla).

She's a Fundamental Christer
    With ALASKA on her keister
    Giving steamin' beamin' McCain a rousing vote of thanks
A suburban soccer moll
    Who hates the urban sprawl
    Of anxious Anchorange and fair Fairbanks

The Governor's Conference in PA
    One swift visit to Se-do-nay
    Are all she knows of the lower 48
Gets a huge amount of fun
    As an NRA top gun
    And there's never been a dead moose
    She would hate

Loves destroying the animal population
    In that ferocious Arctic Nation
    Can't wait to start drilling the chilling Bering Sea
Her love for guns is militaristic
    But her primary characteristic
    Is her verve (right on the nerve) for evangelistic Christianity

Never been to New York or Seattle
    Her greatest diplomatic battle

Is gazing across the Bering Strait
    To Great Siberia
As she's shooting from her stirrup
    There's a chance that all of Europe
    To her, is one totally unknown mysteria

So say hello to Sarah Palin
    New Number One Gal in
    The woman-hating wilderness
    Of the Republican Right
There's no question why McBush
    Took this opportunity to push
    This amazing Chippy-Cheep for Veep.
Man!
    Her plumbing is *sOOOOOOOOOOOOOOOOOO* tight!

So to all you Hillarymaniacs
    Anti-Barack insaniacs
    Here's the New Breed of Maggie Thatcher
    Who'll give us her best shot
As she loads up her AK-47
    Thrusts a virile thumb to Arctic Heaven
She can flaunt her sole endowment
    What a deep Alaskan plow meant for this role:
A pre-menopausal twat.

So Joe Biden's fifty years
    With the little Beltway Dears
Can be dismissed with a peremptory shrug:
Sarah Palin has it all
    As their Christian Party Doll
    With her matching china
    Her Virtuous Vagina
    and her fertile pubic rug.

We wonder if this juicy jerk'll
    Go ten rounds with Angie Merkel

But she sure has Bay Buchanan
            Tootin'…. And deeply rootin'.
From her frozen Juneau shoal
Can she (like GWB) look deep into the soul
            Of sinister Prime Minister Vlad Putin?

O Ignorance! Your innocence is such sweet bliss
When confronted with simple souls such as this
As she thrusts her pubing son "Track" into Iraqi
            Cry & hue
And sits back with John McCain for a tasty helping
            Of moose stew

CRASHING THROUGH THE BRUSH

We fall in worship of fair Sarah Barracuda
Legions of loyal Alaskans have told us to
Even knowing no woman in shoe leather could be cruder
Or more in need of "Taming of the Shrew"
She's up at dawn brandishing her AK-47
Thrashing through the mud and sleet outside divine Wasilla
Lusting for caribou anguish (puts her right in heaven)
And moose blood -- a real, authentic killer-diller
And, **wham! Wham!** She and her lusty brethren breathe the
scent
Of frightened moose in the first light of Arctic dawn
Wham! Wham! Wham! Emblazons their intent
To slaughter every animal they might chance upon

Back in the loins of Greater Metro Wasilla
Hubby Troy polishes all his wife's extra rifles
Watches lustfully as the Ice Hockey King trifles
With ever complaisant equally lustful Bristol
Fuck, man! That redneck hunk is one real pistol!
The other two bumpkins change and burp the feckless brat
With no more intelligence than a baby cat
But, to our immense and fiery indignation
His state has become the catchphrase for this entire nation

We might all model ourselves after this little gnome
We might indeed be all suffering from Down's Syndrome
Aching to elect a woman who doesn't know from squat
Where the only consideration, really, is her twat
All through Alaska there's no more gravid a ratcatcher
She invokes the ghost of damn DameMargaret Thatcher
As helicopter blades roar across the Arctic Circle
She longs to trade ripostes with angry Angela Merkel
For she's been told, in some unknown place that's known as
Yurrup

She might well get her party dress caught in her stirrup

So Sarah Barracuda cozens all her dumb dependents
And crashes through the brush – along with all the man-   boys who
seek Alaskan independence
She and her mighty men can give us all a whack
While her putative son-in-law mingles some grass with
A little Nomic crack
And, for the sake of wanting most to please us
Before they shoot the moose they all kneel down to Jesus
Praising Fair Alaska and her Sons to heaven's skies
Hoping that Arctic Circle sun will burn like hell
As John McCain's carcinoma multiplies

IN OLD ARIZONA

Under the soft red hot Arizona sky
Cindy Hensley was the queen of Phoenix Princessi
She bullied the servants till they cried for Quits
Gave her older sisters conniption fits
Her dad Boss Hensley loved her almost to death
As he covered her with affection and denture breath
Cindy was much more than a shrew and a scold
For Cindy was hung up on everything Old

Cin was never exactly lacking in class
Like the way she cut her sisters off at the pass
Refused to recognize 'em while Pa was in his coffin
Then went lookin' for somethin' Old to be boffin
And before AMTRAK pulled out of the Phoenix yards
Cin cut off her sisters' credit cards

> *Rah! Rah! Cindy and Rah! Rah! Rowdy*
> *You could never say Cindy was dull or dowdy*
> *She could never be described as sizzling tail*
> *Had a mouth like a slot intended for mail*
> *Went about Phoenix dispensing cheer*
> *'Cause Dad had had the corner on Arizona beer*
> *And in the barrooms of Phoenix Cindy huddled*
> *Because she wanted to be coddled and cuddled*

Then from across the bar Cin was poleaxed
God threw Cindy's switches and the Holy Ghost faxed
A message to Cin our Principessa Star
About the very short guy across the bar
Old enough to be her Dad and then some more
Soon our heroine was acting like a tough little whore
Even though his wife Carol was universally respected
Cin soon had his tiny little dick resurrected

Yeah, she fucked John McCain out from under his wife

And prepared to set them both up for a rich kind of life
Was her wedding expensive? Well, I'd say, *Very*
Because beer in Arizona is so necessary
She set her Hanoi Hero up as a congressperson
Soon she had three blond babes to be sucklin and nursin
But Dad's mob connections made all the pickins clean
And John's two grown boys signed on to the Phoenix
    Beer machine

> *Swirl, swirl, Cindy in your cheerleader skirt*
> *Though John left you alone so much it would hurt*
> *But she knew this Old Dad was a ruff kind of man*
> *So she started overdosing Percodan*
> *Even though she was no longer regularly boned*
> *She learned how much fun it was to be totally stoned*

So while John upped and upped from the House to the Senate
Superblond Cindy learned how to take all those gentlemen at
Their word; and as she grew angular and Nancy Reagan thin
She started idly wondering about the shape this world is in
Though her beer bonanza was really funded and run by the Maf
There's never enough Brew for Arizona to quaff
So she turned a blind eye to each Macher and Greaser
And flew off to India and Mother Teresa

Even though she never met the Guru *personally*
Soon Phoenix was filled with stories of how the truth ought to be
She brought back from Pakistan a bundle of joy
McCain didn't have much to say but *Oh, God!* And *Oh, Boy!*
So she added Bridget to her kiddie stables
And sat her family down at nine different tables
Though Cin was a dominant kind of a bitch
What she really was was *filthy rich*

> When John began threatening Dubya-Dub
> Karl Rove cut John out of the Presidential club
> And they cut John out of the Carolina margin

By claiming the Old Boy had been through Pakistan
    Sexually chargin
 Cin was so charmed by this Rovian bloke
She took herself away with a tiny little stroke
Even though having a stroke is kind of a bummer
She acts just like the old babe in "Suddenly Last Summer"

Now she's shakin' But Cin will never be breakin'
On every GOPodium she'll regally stand
Wanting to be the Queen Mother of the land
Dispensing largesse, dissing all that's queer
encouraging everyone to drink Arizona beer
Standing straight and tall Glistening with carats
Endlessly discursing the possible merits
Of that imponderable Alaskan trailer trash
While this whole show is sponsored by Mob
    And Brewski cash

Cindy Rocks! So let the old babe gleam just a bit
Before she falls down in another Percodan fit
Living in all those neighborhoods that are socially restricted
It's no kind of crime to be chemically addicted
Addicted to chems and addicted to power
all set up to be the next Mamie Eisenhower
For in this world of fools and Alaskan fool's gold
It's no sin to be addicted to everything OLD

Old Cindy! Old stepsons! And old, old John
This Presidential Slate has been written upon
As Cindy sets her Slot and, as a nine house owner
Tools her Hummer into the dust of Old Sedona
Looking like a ringer for Cissy Goforth
While the Alaska Barracuda rises like thunder
    In the North

CELEBRITY

Ah the elusive ephemeral concept
    The condition yclept CELEBRITY
It's the turn of the screw that excludes most of you
But because of tell-and-showment
And my considerable endowment
What the man behind the plow meant
Does not exclude me.

Take the case of each dropped stitch
    Of that sleek Alaska bitch
    Temper of turmoil and twitch
    And no desire to please us
When her eldest became, say,
    Ineluctably gay
    She just cast him away
    With a prayer to Jesus
And when Johnston came to shove in
    Bristol's bun in the oven
    She was sent to a Christian coven
    In backstreet Anchorage
But Sister Sarah dropped in her tracks
    When she was knocked to the max
    So she brought poor Bristol bax
    From the Penalty Cage.

    Ah, Celebrity, Republican Celebrity
    Nurtured at the paps of Alaska ur-regnant
    All this Celebrity is shammily
    Sloughed off as "Just Family"
    When these gals hoarily and hammily
    Became publicly pregnant.

Why, in the name of all that's logical
    Can a Peace Corps conception tragical
    Be morphed into something quite magical

And potentially defeatist?
When a man with melting brown lamps
  Raised in Hawaii on food stamps
  Becomes linked with Hollywood tramps
  And considered elitist?
So our man considers this
  And accepts the friendship kiss
  Of Oprah whose celebrity bliss
  Is just curds and no whey
He would never be a harborer
  Of that celebrity known as Barbra
  There's no GOP-goader that's sharperer
  When she blows them all away!

Celebrity, Democratic Celebrity
  A calamitous offshoot
Blasted to the root by New Republic bloggers
Obama should have been a punter
Or an Alaskan wolf hunter
So he might from Fairbanks be trucked
  To be serially shucked
  And ceremonially fucked
  By "Drill, Baby!" loggers

But McCain is Natural Man Himself
  Never to linger on the shelf
  Or to forego any pelf anyone can see
So he gets down with the hand jive
  Of the sleek Keating Five
  And accepts good ol' boy money
  From the beer industry
Cindy whirls in all directions
  With her smart Mob connections
  As McCains seek resurrections
  In some Montenegro play
They endure the rich and rottish
  In Cetinje dance the schottische

With a Neopolitan hottish
And Anne Hathaway.

Oh, inbred well-connected Annapolis trash
You'll criticize Obama for any paltry bash
And then accept the quite corrupted cash
Of the Neapolitan Mob as he climbs on your Bus

So you Plain Folks play Tell-and-Show
And snort some Sicilian blow
In smart EU-friendly Montenegro
And with Anne and her mobster you pass GO
As they both adjust your truss.

THE OLD CAT ROLLS

The old cat rolls around in the sun
Impervious to the wishes of everyone
Grunting at a whiff of a dog in the street
Biting at the talons on his four fat feet
Cuddling and cooing when we stroke his chest
Giving Billy Bedamned about all the rest

Giving Billy Bedamned when Hillary sulks
Billy Bedamned about those Alaskan hulks
If the slut will marry the Ice Hockey King
Or if the Down's-Syndrome infant knows anything
The cat doesn't care if Sarah slaughters a moose
And turns on her sullen husband with its blood
      And its juice
The old cat just rolls around on our sun drenched quilt
And doesn't give a shit – no, not a little bit
      If the Bridge to Nowhere ever gets built

The cat squats in his poop box and makes piss mud
Bites my hand softly and never draws blood
He doesn't care if Cindy is in Mamie Eisenhower mode
Or if John's neck swells till he's about to explode
The cat doesn't care about their multiple lies
Or the soft haze of pollution over Arizona skies
He just worries about warming his ancient bones
And doesn't give squat – no, not a lot
      About how many homes the bitch actually owns

Oh! If independent voters were like our old Tom Cat
But these dweebs never know where their heads are at
Sarah breaking her water can give them a thrill
And they all get hard when John shrieks
      "Drill, Baby, Drill!"
They gaze briefly at Obama and then shy away
Knowing full well he's a lot smarter than they

They'll vote for the old cocker out of laziness and spite
And wonder why the Dude didn't capitalize
      on his mother being white
So we slide messily toward another fray in the balance
Wishing the Man were Dave Petraeus
      Who does pushups like Jack Palance

Trailer Trash is our new Big Noise from Winnetka
So geographically ignorant she thinks Moscow
      Is in Kamchatka
Once again the real issues have been brushed to the side
Proles agonize on poor Bristol
      Who may never be a bride
So the overreaching of the syndrome of this mighty nation
Is not freedom of choice; it's *obfuscation.*

And as the electoral gap becomes wider and wider
Hillary sits in Washington like a black widow spider
Putting blue plumes on her Presidential hat
Rolling in the Patomac sun like an old tabby cat

THE POSE

I like to take my streetside pose
With one foot out and a tilt to my nose
Pretending I'm a cellphone-scofflaw deputy
To all the bad mad drivers that I can see
I strike a deadly pose without a doubt
(with a tilt to my nose and one foot out)
When I see some bitch toolin' along so grand
with a cellphone clutched in her hot little hand
I whip out my own cell and then I pretend
To be dialing the cops and then to send
A message that a scofflaw is in my sight
And should be groveling like a dog in prison tonight

So I pretend to be reading their license plate
Punching in the numbers to seal their fate
Then I beller to the bitch, **Yer breakin' the law**
And I give her a sign with my unoccupied paw
She's been singled out as one bad mad person
And of all scofflaw-drivers
       There's no example worse'n

All this posing went fine till Tuesday at three
When I was standing at Rossmore & Beverly
Saw this chick babbling away on her cell
Waiting at the traffic light to go pell-mell
So I stood right there in my fearless pose
Striking attitude with that "fuck you" tilt to my nose
Punching imaginary numbers into my little phone
Giving the bitch in the car a "fuck you" bone

She scoped out what I was doing and this scofflaw star
Cranked down the window of her bunged-up car
Screamed **son of a bitch** and what is more
She leveled down on me with a handy .44
Giving me no marginal reason for doubt

That to continue her cellphone-fetish
  She would take me out!

Well; being a person with respect for his ass
I hunkered right down on the freshly mown grass
Dropping my cell and, like a grunt in Iraq
I looked for some cover for my freaked-out back
And the bitch chortled with unmitigated glee
At how she had made a real fool out of me

But all over California this sticks in their craw
And they curse Schwarzenegger for this hated new law
Insisting they can drive with foolish intent
Doing any stupid thing they might invent
Buffing their nails; picking their nose
Sloshing hot coffee all over their clothes
Eating yesterday's lunch while reading the Times
Separating their pennies and nickels and dimes
Doing anything but just fucking **drive**
While we wonder how these stupid fuckers
  Are even alive

So I continue to stand with my cell in my hand
Making my presence felt as a reprimand
To these drivers toolin' along in some beat-up car
And what a pain in the butt I really think they are
For when a scofflaw is toolin' along in plain sight
He belongs (like a dog) in some prison tonight
And if they scream or begin to shout bloody murther
I'll just tilt my famous nose up even further
Stick out my foot, and, without another word
Punch in my imaginary message
  And throw them the bird

When first I encountered the blue eyed boy
I was hardly more than an impressionable child
But there was something about this youngman that drove
        This youngerman wild
He was more than a treasure ; less than a toy
Not to be lumped (or lumpen) with the hoi polloi

Never *never* had I seen a man onscreen
Remotely approaching this paragon of beauty
Laboring opposite Virginia Mayo he did
        More than his duty
There was nothing soft about him; always *smart.*
        Always keen
The handsomest fucking Jewboy we'd ever seen

Gravitas; a chiseled face; the body from hell
The Silver Chalice sank without a trace
But none of us could forget that face
Shortly, another epic rang the same bell
A Rocky Graziano biopic? Oh well

We were asked to agree, Somebody Up There Liked Him.
Some bodies Out There certainly did
We all flocked breathlessly
        To patronize this kid
This Theater Devil who addressed our every whim
…and suddenly, we were all obsessed by him

We had to see him in color for the fix to take;
What tied the can to it was *Cat on a Hot Tin Roof*
When we saw those ice-blue eyes
        Every Man Jack of us went **woof**
Yeah. *Brick Pollett* was the role of roles
        Which released the brake
Suddenly our boy was impossible to shake

Nothing kept us from adoring him; now we
　　　Were free to gaze
Unhesitatingly upon that precious face
And to worship that tight body was no mere disgrace
Because *Paul Newman* had become a craze
Releasing us from Brando and Clift
　　　And lazier days

Voluptuous Liz Taylor he could push away
He could embody the lascivious thoughts of Tennessee
Diverging sharply from the used-to-be
Of Gable, Cooper, and emblolden
　　　Hairy thoughts of hairy-chested Holden
　　　Now we were *all* on our merry way
　　　And cinema was in a different day

All of us who knew we were more
　　　Than just a wee bit different
In the straight Eisenhower Society, chafing at the bit
And in the basement of the Pollett mansion
　　　A new match was lit
And we were chomping something much chewier than chives
As blue-eyed Paul faced off against Burl Ives
For us, our boy was more than heaven-sent.

Newman blasted his way into the Pantheon like a rocket.
Great roles fell to him like veritable plums
We agreed: *something more than wicked this way comes*
Then our blue-eyed clever Action Man
Returned to the Broadway stage and Gadge Kazan
Pausing to put another plum role in his pocket

Finally we had the core of the Blue Eyed Boy;
We drooled over the adventures of Chance Wayne
Knowing no one might have courage
　　　To go there again

Bounding, rebounding to deflect his manly rage
Against the lacquered countenance of Miss Page
Re-filling her syringe
        So that we might all enjoy

The hustler hubris of Tennessee's *Sweet Bird*
Then the conjunction we had all anticipated
Came with the marriage to a gal we might have hated
We'd experienced Eve and her *Three Faces*
But Miss Joanne was one of our new graces
So; we whispered, *Newman.*
        And, joined to that: *Woodward.*

For years they conjoined in item after item
We all came out to rally 'round the flag
And, with Lee Remick and Angela filling up the bag
No one could mope that we had seen a bummer
When Paul and Joanne took us on that *Long Hot Summer.*
They were so juicy
        We felt we could bite 'em

Clift fell by the wayside; Brando wallowed into fat
But for the Sixties Paul was Master of the Game
Knocking off *Hud* to maximize his fame
Going nose-to-nose with acting zeal
With always amazing Patricia Neal
And we agreed: *this* is where it's at

Then there was *Harper, Cool Hand Luke,* and *Butch
Cassidy* to round out Paul's escutcheon
Surely there had been no kind of clutch on
This kind of actorly career;
Paul Newman was less than damned
        And more than dear
And, throbbing, sobbing
        We all released *that* clutch.

He and Bob Redford sailed, so together, off that cliff
We suspected the Worst; prayed for it, actually
That this kind of intensity could exist
   Between He and He
Then super-epics became the Seventies thing
And *Towering Inferno* outpaced *The Sting*
As our boy tried out another acting riff

SUPERSTAR. But there was so much more to him
   Than that
As his career dissipated into chunks
Of meaty fare like *Fort Apache, the Bronx*
Absence of Malice yet another grail
And *The Verdict* convinced us our Man could not fail
But we saw (for the first time) rings of sweat
   Around his hat

Is *Paul Newman* possibly getting old?
But no one could suggest a course so dampling
As he progressed from Sally Field
   To Charlotte Rampling
And then, to generate the newest Newman's pet
He marketed his own brand of vinaigrette
Best served lukewarm; but even better cold

Color of Money was the reward for all which
   Had gone before
And in a crazy kind of actor-attrition
He rounded out his film career on that
   Road to Perdition
Sending Tom Hanks to his grave with that killer's smile
Knowing he could be this kind of bastard all the while
Never quite wholesome, but never, *never*
   Just another acting whore.

We last saw him on the Showtime special *Iconoclasts*
Leading Bob Redford through the bosky dells of

Connecticut
Then we Newman-fanciers knew
            Deep in our gut
Since we had spent fifty years worshipping this friend
All of us were afraid to write: THE END
Because Paul Newman is a pleasure
            Which always lasts.

WE GO WAY UP

In the days when Ottoman Pashas were holding back the Rus
There was a man named Bajazet who would not get off the bus
And of all the Rough Trade in Istanbul no one was more
      Mano a mano
Than Bajazet's main opponent   a dude named Tamerlano
When they finally clashed on the blood soaked straits
      Between Old Asia and New Europe
Bajazet got caught in his traces and dangled from

Tamerlane's bloody stirrup

While Bajazet was croaking   full of misery and pain
Tamerlane sneered with a frown,
Man, you've gone way down
And you won't go up again

So we go way up and we go way down
And the way to exact this Stingo
Is that in our time   these dudes in their prime
Are played by Dave Daniels and Placido Domingo!
So to be a big boss rooster you also have to play the henner
Or, at the very least, be a versatile beast
Or a full scale dramatic tenor.

Teddy Roosevelt was a sissy of the most dissatisfied kind
Mr Ted was a loaded spring
      About to unwind
Ted worked out with freeweights   Pumped his chest
      Real big
Ran around with all the gun buffs   But he was still one ugly pig
And despite the fact he was rough and quite ungainly
He got elected Vice Prez under skinny old William McKinley
When the assassin came and popped the Prez   Ted was riding
      High on the hog
And Cousin Franklin developed polio. Now who was bottom dog?
Teddy mounted his horse   Rode up San Juan Hill   despite
      All those Cuban germs

But Franklin rode even higher on the Grand Old Hog
    And was Prez for four unprecedented terms!

So Teddy went way up and he went way down
And his daughter Alice Blue
Found two dozen ways to dun the willing GOP
In a fem manner tried and true
While Franklin watched from his wheelchair
Their cousin Eleanor (also his wife)
Advanced the pursuit of every Democratic beaut
And extolled the lesbian life.

Dick Nixon made his way out of Whittier Cal
With a five o' clock shadow so black
And he waved the flag of Communist Menace
Chased Helen Douglas out of the shack
Rode into office behind Smilin' Ike
Supported by inebriated Gracious Pat
He went running around the Washington Merry-Go-Round
Pointing out where Jack Kennedy had shat
But Jack had the looks and lovely Jackie
To make his way into Higher Office
And Nixon had to make *his* way to Watergate
To find hideous new ways to boff us!

Tricky Dick went up and he went way down
And Pat drank him into penury
But he sailed like a breeze into China Seas
Under sail of HMS Kissinger (Henry)
Jack nailed Marilyn and Gene Tierney in the
       Lincoln Bedroom
With all the techniques he had hoarded
Then he got into scenes with Marlene Dietrich
And all those chicks got waterboarded!

W got born in Connecticut to a family of political whores
And his Mom Bar B for all to see was a game

That no one scores
Poppy Bush took his tribe to Texass   and unlike
          Ronnie or Rudy
Proceeded to despoil on all things OIL   and all gentlemen
          Saudi
As all this trash was about to crash
          Bar lifted her paws to heaven
And with a thankful scoop from Poppy's Carlyle Group
          They manufactured 9/11.
So W made his way into the Highest Office with percentage
          Points lofty and sound
But now the son of a bitch is right down in the ditch
          With his fur belly draggin' the ground

So Georgie went way up and he went way down
With Dick Cheney whipping his flanks
And they took a right tack into downtown Iraq
With no armament on their tanks
So he's on his way back to Crawford
And he has passed his leadership baton
To a son of a pain known as John McCain
And that disgusting Alaskan spawn

Go way up! Go way down! And never learn a thing
Sing a song of American Values   and let the rafters ring
Climb on the sled with Tamerlane and Bajazet
      Who never got off the bus
And grope around down there for John's tiny dick
And adjust his pathetic truss

THRILLED

Thrilled.

Thrilled to the marrow of my old bones
Thrilled to be alive and conscious in this Brave New World
Where a black man has been elected President
      Of these United States
Without once pointing the finger
      At his white mother or white grandparents

Thrilled

To see the bastions of the Old South
      North Carolina   Florida even Indiana
Fall into the maw of the New Order

Thrilled to see the razor thin event in Missouri
      Where Jayhawkers once lynched black men for sport

Thrilled to see proto-Mormon Nevada fall
      Casinos of Vegas and Reno must be using
      Blue chips for their exclusive currency

Thrilled to see Michelle Obama
      Stride that stage in Chicago with the aplomb
      Of a woman born to understand power
      And not to abuse it
As grim slash-mouthed Cindy
      Lets Joe Lieberman in for his boyish drooling kiss
      While he and John-Boy share their crocodile tears
      As if she cared

Thrilled that Sarah Barracuda will be returning to Juneau
      To face an unthrilled population
      Of disenchanted Alaskans

Thrilled that Obama's caring grandmother Evelyn
    Who gave up her muumuus for bank president's power garb
    Who brought up her half-Kenyan grandson with dignity and
wisdom
    Almost lived to see her handsome charge be elected President
    And still they criticized him
        For returning to Hawaii

Thrilled that last minute robo-calls in Florida
    Proclaiming Castro had given Obama his dotard blessing
    Were seen through as so much bullshit
    By the new Cuban American voters
    Who finally sorted out who their real friends are

Thrilled that I have got past Nixon and his threatening five o'clock
shadow
Got past my horror at how the gullible populace rejected Jimmy
Carter
    A truly great President with heart and vision
Got past Ronnie and his inability to sort out where Reykjavik really is
Got past Poppy Bush and his wonder at the reality of bar codes
Got past the messy spectacle of the Clintons
    Their inbred envy of each other   Toxic to the max
Got past Junior and his eight years of total debacle on every level

Thrilled to be past all that
Never forgetting a thing
We'll need long memories for perspective
as we enter Terra Incognita
Shaking and trembling